Ex's & Oh's

Dealing with Parental Alienation
and Healing Through the Pain

J.K. Nation

WESTBOW
PRESS®
A DIVISION OF THOMAS NELSON
& ZONDERVAN

Copyright © 2019 J.K. Nation.

All rights reserved. No part of this book may be used or reproduced by any means, graphic, electronic, or mechanical, including photocopying, recording, taping or by any information storage retrieval system without the written permission of the author except in the case of brief quotations embodied in critical articles and reviews.

Scripture taken from The Message. Copyright © 1993, 1994, 1995, 1996, 2000, 2001, 2002. Used by permission of NavPress Publishing Group.

THE HOLY BIBLE, NEW INTERNATIONAL VERSION®, NIV® Copyright © 1973, 1978, 1984, 2011 by Biblica, Inc.® Used by permission. All rights reserved worldwide.

Scripture taken from the New King James Version®. Copyright © 1982 by Thomas Nelson. Used by permission. All rights reserved.

Scripture taken from the NEW AMERICAN STANDARD BIBLE®, Copyright © 1960,1962, 1963,1968,1971,1972,1973,1975,1977,1995 by The Lockman Foundation. Used by permission.

WestBow Press books may be ordered through booksellers or by contacting:

WestBow Press
A Division of Thomas Nelson & Zondervan
1663 Liberty Drive
Bloomington, IN 47403
www.westbowpress.com
1 (866) 928-1240

Because of the dynamic nature of the Internet, any web addresses or links contained in this book may have changed since publication and may no longer be valid. The views expressed in this work are solely those of the author and do not necessarily reflect the views of the publisher, and the publisher hereby disclaims any responsibility for them.

Any people depicted in stock imagery provided by Getty Images are models, and such images are being used for illustrative purposes only.
Certain stock imagery © Getty Images.

ISBN: 978-1-9736-5958-7 (sc)
ISBN: 978-1-9736-5960-0 (hc)
ISBN: 978-1-9736-5959-4 (e)

Library of Congress Control Number: 2019904180

Print information available on the last page.

WestBow Press rev. date: 04/22/2019

Contents

Introduction vii

1. "Is This My Reality?" 1
2. The Crossfire of Divorce and Parental Alienation 15
3. The Effects of Parental Alienation on the Extended Family 34
4. Loving Your Child from a Distance 48
5. What Did You Say? 63
6. How Do I Deal with the Pain and Heal Properly? 74
7. Praying and Seeking Restoration in the Home 88
8. Talking About Forgiveness 101
9. Starting New Goals and Dreams 116

Acknowledgements 133
About the Author 135

Introduction

When I set out to write *Ex's & Oh's*, I needed to reconcile where God was leading me and if there is a solution to the brokenness I felt when my marriage imploded and our marital union became another divorce statistic. After a long, dark period, I experienced a long journey of healing, tears, and hope, and I want to share what I experienced and what I learned on these pages.

To understand the passion that has driven me to share my story, I must take you back to the fall of 2008 when I was in the construction design field, drawing up plans and designs for everything from small residential additions to large commercial projects. Just as the Great Recession was gaining steam, the housing market took a major hit. In just a few short months, my design company lost nearly a quarter of a million dollars as my clients failed to pay. I had to shut down my business and file for bankruptcy. We lost everything. If that wasn't bleak enough, the only asset we could protect from bankruptcy—our home—was damaged by a tropical storm.

I was married to Rachel, which is a pseudonym.[1] We had been married at the time for twelve years and were raising four children from the ages of six to eleven. Because of the disastrous financial losses, we had to move from our beautiful home into a tight three-bedroom apartment. The trauma took a heavy toll on my family and my marriage. During this time, I suffered from several health issues, which limited the amount of work I

---

[1] For legal reasons, I must use a pseudonym as well. J.K. Nations is not my real name.

could do. My wife had to re-enter the work force after being a stay-at-home mother for nearly twelve years, which changed the family dynamics.

In November 2009, our marriage sunk and ended in an ugly divorce after I found out that my wife had an affair with a colleague at her new place of work.

During one of my restless nights, I was praying and talking to God, telling Him that I was broken to the point where I felt like I was crushed into powder.

He responded back to my spirit, saying, *Although you may be powder, you do not know that you are exactly where I need you to be. You see, when something is broken, it has its limitations on how it can be used. It is either restored to the same thing or as something different with the same elements. When something that was has been ground to powder though, only then can I add My healing water and make it into something new where it doesn't even resemble what it once was.*

Over the past several years, I have appeared before four separate judges in two different states with nearly one hundred hearings. Most of these court appearances had to do with custody issues with my children. To get what she wanted, my ex-wife moved halfway across the country, making it much more difficult for me to see the children. Because of the separation and alienation from my kids, I embarked on an emotional roller-coaster ride and wondered how many other parents were going through what was happening to me.

I've since come to understand that I experienced something known as Parental Alienation. If you've ever been through a divorce, with custody matters, then you know what I'm talking about. Parental Alienation takes a toll physically and emotionally. When meeting a parent alienated from his or her children, one may think the parent is telling outlandish stories riddled with exaggeration or lies. Some may even think the parent has a mental illness. Many who struggle with Parental Alienation or PA suffer from depression or experience PTSD-like symptoms because of their trauma. Some even commit suicide due to their loss.

While the pain of divorce is difficult, the intense pain of being separated from your children is debilitating. For me, it felt like wave after wave and tragedy after tragedy to a point where I could not breathe or get out of bed in the morning.

Bluntly said, Parental Alienation happens when your former spouse takes your children, your finances, and then every last shred of your hope. Most people who have gone down this path have lost everything—their personal belongings, their relationships, their homes, and in some cases even their families. They are left alone like a ship on a vast sea in the darkness with no lighthouse to guide them.

In addition, the alienating parent plays the victim card and rallies people around them to demonize the other parent. They may gain a lot in the short run, but the damage they cause to family members is devastating.

As the pendulum swings from one extreme to the other, there are many who suffer collateral damage from this turbulent battle. Extended family can suffer greatly as they lose out on relationships with the children (or grandchildren in some cases), but the ones most affected are the children that both parents are fighting for. As one of my sons said to me, "Dad, you have no idea how much this [divorce] has affected me. I didn't sign up for this. All I wanted was a normal life!"

Children, who look for stability and consistency from their parents, will give their loyalty to the one who gives them strength and security. They want to freely love both parents as they please but they don't want to get into the drama of what their parents are dealing with.

I took all of this into account during my most difficult days and asked myself if there is a biblical solution to this great problem of Parental Alienation following a bitter divorce. I felt led to study two specific verses:

> "A thief is only there to steal and to kill and destroy. I came so they can have real and eternal life, more and better life than they ever dream of."
> —John 10:10 (MSG)

> "Believe me: I am in my Father and my Father is in me. If you can't believe that, believe what you see—these works. The person who trusts me will not only do what I'm doing but even greater things, because I, on my way to the Father, am giving you the same work to do that I've been doing. You can count on it. From now on, whatever you request along the lines of who I am and what I am doing, I'll do it. That's how the Father will be seen for

who he is in the Son. I mean it. Whatever you request in this way, I'll do."

—John 14:11-14 (MSG)

These two Scriptures greatly encouraged me with a reminder that all of us dealing with PA have been called out to give hope. In our obedience and pressing into God's fullness in our dark times, He has given us the ability not just to overcome things, but to speak life and healing into the brokenness of others.

It's easy to get caught up in the past, so when I went through divorce and separation from my kids, I felt like I was looking through a mirror. The truth is that after the divorce, I tried to live in the past with the things that defined who my family was. These elements consisted of our geographic location, the favorite activities that I did with my family, and being involved in the children's school activities.

As the years are passed by, though, it was easy to look in the mirror of my past as a way to define how my future should look. I assumed that looking at the reflection was my reality, but some objects in a mirror are "closer than they appear," as we sometimes see in car mirrors. The truth is when you look in a mirror, you find that the things you have been holding dear are further away than you think and are going to stay that way, which means you have to deal with things the way they are.

It can be difficult to accept this reality, which is why it's important to be close to God and let Him guide you along this difficult journey.

God reminds you to set your eyes on the prize ahead so that you may finish the race set before you (Philippians 3:12-14). Although my life has been really tough since the divorce, I've learned that what I'm going through right now does not define the promises and future ahead.

Too often, as I discovered, I couldn't see beyond the pain. I often asked myself, "God, what is next?" At first, the question posed itself in a negative light, but as I sought God in the darkest valley, the question went from a negative to a positive as I looked to the Lord for what's next.

Although the journey I've been on has been difficult, God has shown me many distinct aspects of His goodness. For instance, when I changed my perspective, I could see some important things that helped me get through the darkest of valleys. One of the greatest lessons was gaining a fuller understanding of Psalm 23 and how God was with me every step of the way. I need not need to fear evil.

While writing this book, God showed me the true meaning of Psalm 23's six verses and how important they were to overcoming the traumatic experiences I went through. The fifth verse, in particular, spoke to me:

> You prepare a table before me
> in the presence of my enemy.
> —Psalm 23:5 (NIV)

Too often in a traumatic experience, like death or divorce, it's easy to focus on your troubles than it is on the table that God has laid out before you.

Likewise, God's blessings can be missed if you do not trust Him enough to take care of the things happening to you and the emotions you're experiencing. The table is set for your nourishment and enjoyment, but it is up to you to explore all the goodness God has set before you while not allowing yourself to be distracted by things that are out of your control.

I've written *Ex's & Oh's* because I want to help you hit the reset button and start life all new again with a hope and a future. When you love yourself the way God loves you, you can pour that into your children and future generations. What I'm sharing here is made with *you* in mind so that you can experience God in a new and fresh way, as this Scripture reminds us:

> "For I know the plans I have for you," declares the Lord, "plans to prosper you and not to harm you, plans to give you hope and a future."
> —Jeremiah 29:11 (NIV)

So thanks for joining me. If you or someone close to you has experienced the gut-wrenching loss of a marriage and being alienated from your children, then you've come to the right place.

1
"Is This My Reality?"

Divorce is a hideous thing, but being separated from your children or grandchildren following a marital breakup produces pain that is unimaginable. The hurtful messages left on my cell phone, the distressing texts, and the demeaning things said in the courtroom really threw me for a loop.

I always thought that being a father of four children was a blessing, but after my divorce, I never thought I would experience a fraction of unbearable pain that I did. There were times when I wondered, *What did I miss being married to this other person, only to have her to turn on me in such a mean way?*

If you've gone through something like this, then you know what I'm talking about. The aftermath of divorce can churn out the greatest emotional pain that anyone could possibly experience, especially when children are involved. It's one thing for a spouse or a judge to keep you from your children, but it's a completely different thing when your children believe the lies fed to them—outright falsehoods told by your ex that prompt these innocent creatures to treat you with disrespect and reject you as a parent.

I have plenty of personal examples to draw upon. For instance, one of my children was born on my birthday, so it was always a joy to share such a special day with him. After my divorce, though, this happy occasion was used again me like a vise. My ex poisoned the well so much in the days leading up to our shared birthday that when the children arrived at the restaurant, they were unhappy because of all the stress they were feeling from the lies my ex told about me. My oldest son and youngest son were happy to see me, but my other two children were so reserved in their emotions that I could tell that something had been said about me their mother—and it wasn't warm and loving.

From the moment I met the children at an Italian restaurant to celebrate our birthdays, I detected their distress, but I did my best to keep everything on an even keel because I had not seen my children in two months. (That's another story.) But here's the clincher: during our dinner, my ex took the liberty to blow up my phone as well as my oldest son's phone with a lot of unnecessary texts in an attempt to ruin the evening for us, like demanding to pick them up sooner than we had agreed upon as part of our visitation agreement. Then she showed up at the restaurant early, which created a scene that you can only imagine.

This would not be the last time she pulled stunts like this; I can cite many other examples. She threatened the children on occasion, promising them certain things and special gifts in exchange for not showing me respect and honor as their father. I can't tell you the number of times the police were called on me during our visits because of baseless accusations that I was mistreating the children.

One time, my boys came over the house. We decided to make a late breakfast. Within ten minutes, just as we were pouring pancake batter on the griddle, we heard a loud pounding at my front door. My oldest son said, "Here we go again! Mom called the cops on Dad. What did he do this time?"

Episodes like that reminded me that my life was ruled by chaos. It was during these turbulent times that I wondered, "Is this my reality?" All too sadly, it was.

Most people who go through divorce experience a wave of emotion, while those who get divorced with children end up going through multiple waves of emotions. They feel like the bumpy ride will never end, and that there is no hope anywhere in sight.

That's certainly how I felt.

> "In every encounter, we either give life or drain it; there is no neutral exchange. We enhance human dignity, or we diminish it.'
> —Brennan Manning, author of *The Ragmuffin Gospel*

This is why I want to talk about Parental Alienation and to assure you that you are not alone. You have plunged into a journey that is surreal to yourself and unbelievable to others.

If I could describe to anyone the difference between going through a divorce and going through a divorce with children, it would be the intensity of the storm—and the frequency. A simple divorce would be like a storm that blew off your roof and created much damage to your home. Sure, fixing the damage would be costly and take some time, but you will eventually recover and go on with life. A divorce when there are children involved is a much different tempest—like the difference between a Nor'easter and a Category 5 hurricane. Child can and often become pawns in the divorce proceedings.

When I went through my divorce, I never thought in a million years that the dissolution of my marriage would inflict the damage that it did or cause the pain that knocked me over, as well as what they paid did to my four children and our family and friends. As I picked up the pieces after the hurricane passed though, another Cat 5 hit me me—only to be followed up by another major tropical storm. The reality is that the pain, exhaustion, sorrow, and loss were so indescribable that that unless you've been through it, no one will really understand what knocks your world upside down.

If you're going through a divorce or are headed in that direction, let me start with several exercises that I want you to do. Here's the first one:

1. **Identify your feelings.**

Begin by reading this Scripture:

> Sing praise to the Lord, you His godly ones,
> And give thanks to His holy name.
> For His anger is but for a moment,

His favor is for a lifetime;
Weeping may last for the night,
But a shout of joy comes in the morning.
—Psalm 30:4-5 (NASB)

Next, I want to reflect on your feelings after reading this psalm. Can you identify personally with any of these feelings? If so, write down your thoughts here:

_____

_____

_____

_____

_____

_____

When you're a divorced parent, your feelings can vary from one extreme to another. In the space below, be honest with yourself and write down how you are feeling right now. Understand that being angry enough with your ex-spouse to wish harm on her (or him) is not uncommon but is unhealthy in the long term. You may want to seek out counseling to help you get through this healing process.

_____

_____

_____

_____

_____

_____

Are you able to refrain from speaking ill about your ex-spouse to your children or to those who could relay what they heard to your ex? That's something you want to be careful about. In the space below, give some examples of how you can speak kindly to your children about their other parent and extended family.

_____

_____

_____

_____

Children are smarter and more attuned to what is going on than you think. Have you shared anything with your children (age appropriate, of course) about what's going on in the disillusion process or divorce court proceedings? Below, list some of the things you have shared with them, or items they may have overheard and how it may have affected them in an adverse way.

_____

_____

_____

_____

Too often we allow our feelings to dictate our actions. When we are happy, we may want to do something good for someone. When we are angry, though, we tend to do something destructive, which brings about more pain. It's human nature to wish the same hurts and pain on the one who caused it.

Regardless what your spouse has done to you or to your children to spite you, please understand that you have no control over anything but how you react. Everything may be a big blur with distractions from endless court documents, visits from police, interviews with the DCF (Department of Children and Family), or hearing false accusations from people who you thought were your friends, but you have to keep your wits about you.

What hurts the most is to receive hurtful accusations from your sons and daughters. Remember your children are just that—children—and they are trying to make sense of this thing just like you are, but they have less life experiences to draw upon. They are hurting, too, but keep in mind that their bruised feelings could be in a greater magnitude because their security has just been swept out from under them.

2. **Don't be afraid to speak life into your situation, meaning don't be afraid to talk about having hope and security in the situation. Doing this is a way for you, as the parent, to protect your children by showing them how to find strength in tragedy.**

Begin by reading this Scripture:

> A brother wronged is more unyielding than a fortified city; disputes are like the barred gates of a citadel.
> From the fruit of their mouth a person's stomach is filled; with the harvest of their lips they are satisfied.
> The tongue has the power of life and death, and those who love it will eat it's fruit.
> —Proverbs 18:19-21 (NIV)

Speaking life into a situation can be difficult when you feel like you've been fully betrayed by the person you have entrusted with your marriage and your children. But you have to be willing to directly address the situation you're in.

It also helps when those close to you can be honest. At the onset of my divorce, I had a dear friend who challenged me to eat right and start exercising. Because I was fighting depression, I lost more than fifty pounds and couldn't do anything much more than sleep, read books, and pour my heart out to God about my bleak situation. My friend offered to help out even though he did not know the pain I was going through or even about the separation of my children, but one thing he did understand was what it meant to live a healthy life—physically, mentally, emotionally, and spiritually. At the time, I saw how strong a man of God he was and felt I could learn something from him.

Under his encouragement, I spent many hours walking, talking to God and journaling those conversations. On many occasions, recording my innermost feelings on paper required me to shed many tears. I found myself looking forward to my two-hour walks while listening to praise and worship music, praying, and just listening to God. The twilight walks through the neighborhood were a great replacement for all the evenings I would cry myself to sleep over my wife leaving me and turning my children against me.

I had to resolve to leave a desolate place ravaged by loss and betrayal. If it weren't for my dear friend being there for me and listening to where God was leading me, I would never be at the place I am today.

Exercises:

- Have you found a way to speak life into your journey? In what way have you done so?

_____

_____

_____

- Have you put yourself around others who will listen and talk to you about your journey of divorce and separation with your children/grandchildren? List a few people you can trust to help you and speak life into you. (Be careful, though, about asking other family or mutual friends that you and your ex-spouse may have had together. They may be overly biased in one way or another and can sway your feelings as a result.)

- What activities have you done—or are doing—that would allow you a quiet time to seek God and distance yourself from the turmoil you're experiencing? Identify some healthy habits that you did *not* do while you were married, such as exercising, doing service for someone else, or simply slowing down enough to enjoy what life has to offer.

Ex's & Oh's

_____
_____
_____
_____

- What music are you listening to? Do you listen to praise and worship songs to get your focus on God and keep your mind captive on your loss? List four songs making a positive impact on your thinking and a couple of songs that had a negative impact on your thinking and mood.

_____
_____
_____
_____
_____

- In Brennan Manning's quote about giving life or draining it in every encounter, what would you say were the good and bad aspects about your marriage? With your children?

_____
_____
_____

_____

_____

Challenge:

One thing I found to be extremely beneficial was to journal, which is something I rarely did while I was married. When a close friend encouraged me to give it a try, I did not realize the course that journaling would set me on.

When I started to write down my thoughts, I zeroed in on the wrongs my ex did to me, as well as others. I viewed their actions as an injustice and outlined them on paper. As time went on, after I got past my venting, I found that my writing became an introspective view of who I am. My relationship with God deepened with each written page.

I urge you to buy a journal or notebook. Whenever you are mad, optimistic, angry, or hopeful about the future, write those thoughts down. You will be surprised what you will learn about yourself.

Then bow your head and whisper a prayer like this:

God, I know we are not perfect, but with that said, show me how You see me. Allow my words to bring life to those I meet as well as my children and in my life. Allow me to see Your bigger picture and not the journey that is ahead. Keep my eyes focused on you. In Christ's name, amen.

Here are some additional Scriptures to dwell on:

> But no human being can tame the tongue. It is a restless evil, full of deadly poison. With the tongue we praise our Lord and Father, and with it we curse human beings, who have been made in God's likeness. Out of the same mouth come praise and cursing. My brothers and sisters, this should not be. Can both fresh water and salt water flow from the same spring? My brothers and sisters, can a fig tree bear olives, or a grapevine bear figs? Neither can a salt spring produce fresh water.
>
> —James 3:8-12 (NIV)

> My dear brothers and sisters, take note of this: Everyone should be quick to listen, slow to speak and slow to become angry.
> —James 1:19 (NIV)

> "Be angry and do not sin": do not let the sun go down upon your wrath.
> —Ephesians 4:26 (NKJV)

> You've kept track of my every toss and turn
>   through the sleepless nights,
> Each tear entered in your ledger,
>   each ache written in your book.
> —Psalm 56:8 (MSG)

Look at Job's journey. He lost everything, yet because he endured God restored to him everything in greater abundance.

Take some time to journal your thoughts on what you've read so far and strategies that would be helpful to implement:

_____

_____

_____

_____

_____

_____

_____

_____

2

The Crossfire of Divorce and Parental Alienation

> "When you get into a tight place and everything goes against you, till it seems as though you could not hang on a minute longer, never give up then, for that is just the place and time that the tide will turn."
> —Harriet Beecher Stowe, 19th century author

The journey of divorce may seem like a battle with an ex-spouse and the courts over material items, custody issues, child support, and so on, but unless you've been through a marital breakup, it's a battle beyond one's imagination. Unfortunately, most who experience parental alienation and custody issues do not understand the full scope of what they're going through, often because they're too busy putting out spot fires when they should realize the entire forest is in flames.

Before you can fully understand what you're up against, you must realize that at least three fires will likely pop up and contribute to the alienation with your children—and each will be used against you by your ex. The first fire is most obvious, which is the physical and spiritual battle you're engaged in, even though the spiritual battle is less obvious. The second fire is the mental and health battles that you're facing, and the final one is the financial battle. Everyone who has gone through Parental Alienation can attest to these three types of battles. Sometimes they merge together to form one really huge forest fire. Let me explain a little more.

After my separation, I was forced into hiring an attorney. I didn't know much about the legal system, divorce law, or who to hire, especially because I needed to engage an out-of-state divorce attorney as well as have one in my home state.

I called a friend of mine who happened to be a lawyer, even though his specialty was not family law. I gave him a brief synopsis of what was going on and how my ex was acting. After quietly listening, he advised me to avoid going to court at any cost, especially the out-of-state court that my ex-wife was seeking as a change of venue.

I know that this may be a bit complex to follow as there were five separate judges in two different states adjudicating the divorce and visitation proceedings. I can assure you that each jurist had an important role in either perpetuating the environment of Parental Alienation or seeing the need for both parents to be involved in the lives of the children in a healthy way.

The most interesting comment came from Judge 1 in my home state. In the late fall of 2009, Judge No. 1 heard my wife accuse me of domestic violence and describe those actions as being the major reason she wanted to end our marriage. During the hearing, the judge looked at my wife and said, "Ma'am, I know you may want to leave your marriage, and I see that there is contention between you and your husband, but I must caution you, seeing that you have four young children that need the both of you in their lives. Before you embark on a course of action, I want you to take your children into account first because what you decide will affect them for a lifetime. I would also like the both of you to get counseling and work toward reconciling with each other for the benefit of the children. Because of the apparent tension in your relationship, however, I suggest a cooling-off period. Therefore, I am issuing an order that either of you will be arrested if there is any kind of mistreatment or aggressive behavior from either of you. This order of the court will expire in one year."

During that first year, my estranged wife began plotting her plan. She shifted money out of our joint bank accounts and deposited the funds into her new personal account and took steps to make sure I could not get access to the children's medical records and educational documents (news of field trips, report cards, etc.). All this was done without my knowledge. She also called the police each time the children visited my new home in an attempt to harass me.

Her most grievous action happened the following spring when she told me that she wanted to take the kids to visit a sick family member several states away and would be back in a couple weeks. She never did return. Instead, she and the kids took up residence in this other state, which was a thousand miles away. Before she left, though, she filed for divorce and packed up everything we owned and locked up our stuff in a storage unit,

Ex's & Oh's

taking what she wanted to her new home in another state and telling the children I took everything from them.

It got worse. Before the original order expired, she petitioned Judge No. 1 to extend his order, hoping that she could keep the kids from me indefinitely up to and beyond the dissolution hearing. Then I was contacted by the local sheriff's office about her outlandish claims of abuse and how she was looking for a permanent restraining order. After discussing the situation with the chief of police and describing my side of the story, he decided to issue an order for her arrest for making false claims.

Judge No. 2 blocked that order, however. Instead, he issued a dissolution decree stating that the children would reside with my ex in the new state while granting me one weekend visit per month, all at my expense. This was in addition to the monthly child support that I was ordered to pay. Not only did the judge's actions wipe me out financially, but living more than a thousand miles apart made it very difficult for me to exercise my parental visitation rights.

Judge No. 2, a man, did call out my ex about her attempt to block me from seeing my kids, however. "I don't see any grounds to revoke his parental rights," he said. "I think only allowing Mr. Nation the opportunity to see his kids once a month with no overnights is pretty extreme, don't you think?"

She was greatly offended by his ruling and debated the judge until she saw she wasn't going to win and backed off. Once we left the courtroom, however, she defied the judge's ruling anyway and refused to allow me to visit the children on five occasions *or* talk to them on the phone. My ex was paving the road to Parental Alienation.

Her next legal maneuver was to accuse me of child and domestic abuse before a third judge and serve me papers only ten days before Judge No. 2 was to hear matters of contempt. Her goal was to preempt that claim and eliminate my parental rights so she could move on with her life and end my relationship with the children.

This led me into the courtroom of Judge No. 3, presiding over the court in the state that she had taken our kids to. She felt that she could get what she wanted with Judge No. 3, but the judge felt she was way off base and sided with me, keeping the previous order intact.

"Ma'am, I do not understand *how* your ex-husband could have abused you or your children when he lives a thousand miles away. That makes no sense to me. If you feel there are matters pertaining to the best interests of the children, then you will have to take the case back to the original state, where they have jurisdiction. You will have to petition the court there to sort things out or ask them to transfer the case here."

That wasn't going to work for my ex-wife. Two months later, she had a different judge from the same court hear the case, even though the law contends that jurisdiction belongs in the home state. After Judge No. 4, who was handpicked by my ex-wife, heard the case, he gave her everything she wanted while ignoring everything that had happened over the previous twenty-five months. But this wasn't enough blood. She decided to involve a *fifth* judge, this time in our home state, in an attempt to extract more child support from me.

As my friend said, *Stay out of court at all costs*, but there was no way that was going to happen. After more than five years, 350 filings, and more than seventy-five trips to court, I would say that I've gone through the wringer. The biggest thing I learned is that the U.S. legal system is certainly not the place you want to be when sorting out the dissolution of marriage, especially when children are involved.

I'm afraid my legal battles are not over. I have been put into a position where I have to continue to fight for my parental visitation rights so that I can see my children and be as much as a father as I can be to them. This fight is not about me but about me exercising my parental rights, and I intend to see it through.

I am my children's father, and I want a relationship with them, no matter what my ex says about me. Although this may seem like a physical battle with my ex and the courts, I realize there is a spiritual battle going on as well. This battle has to do with the legacy God is handing down, from generation to generation, to see His plans worked out in my life, the lives of my children, and the lives of their children. If the devil can sow seeds of contention, doubt, rejection, and loss of hope, he feels he can change the trajectory of what God has in store to do through us for His Kingdom.

Exercise #1:

How do you avoid taking matters to court and lower the temperature after a marital separation? How do you have a divorce court sort things out correctly, especially when children are involved and one of the adults is being unreasonable and trying to shut you out of being part of the children's lives?

The first thing to do is consult Scripture. An applicable verse from the Bible is this:

> For our struggle is not against flesh and blood, but against the rulers, against the authorities, against the powers of this dark world and against the spiritual forces of evil in the heavenly realms.
> —Ephesians 6:12 (NIV)

This Scripture reminds me there is a spiritual battle going on because Satan *loves* to split up families and get parents fighting with each other. He knows how much damage that does to everyone involved, especially the children and their future.

So I ask you: Do you understand the battle you're in? Do you understand that there are spiritual forces at work here?

Write down some things that you have experienced in the court or done by your ex. Then take those items and look at them from a spiritual standpoint and see how they may have a long-term effect on both your future and the future of your children. Write down some encouraging thoughts to come back to when experiencing the court battles and arguments with your ex. These may be a verse, a lyrics to a song, or a promise that you can hold on to.

_____

_____

_____

_____

_____

I know that I had to learn to step back and take a different view in my legal battles over the years. God has been showing me that there is more than one perspective to everything we see. It's easy to fight against the injustice to the point where the children seem to be on the back burner, but I now see that I require a different approach and perspective about why I'm entrenched in this battle and how to navigate through it properly.

During one of my Skype visits with my children, my second son said something extremely profound in his ten-year-old self. "Dad, I didn't sign up for this," he said, referring to the divorce. "All I want is a normal life."

This one comment from my son has changed my perspective on the riff between my ex-wife and me. His words showed me that although I'm fighting against injustice, for my reputation and relationships with my children, there is much more going on here. I also realized that although there were things happening to me that were wrong, I had come to the understanding that it was happening in the same measure to innocent children who were far less prepared to deal with the trauma than an adult like myself. Children look for the stability in their home to thrive, but when that is affected by a trauma such as divorce, they start questioning if there is any hope for their futures. When there is no hope, that can cause them to act out.

In the space below, write down how your actions and thinking may be adversely effecting your children. Look at what's been happening from a physical approach as well as the spiritual impact it may have on your children.

_____

_____

_____

_____

_____

_____

Everything going on around us is a result of a spiritual battle, and we may not even see it. When going into war, the general creates a battle plan and has a contingency plan of action. Any battle, whether fought on the field or in the court, always needs a plan. Write down your course of action for the divorce.

After you have written this out, first ask God to show you the flaws of your battle plan. Then give a copy of your plan to a close friend or counselor, who can scrutinize your ideas and offer suggestions. Above all, seek a God-honoring approach, not a scorched earth policy. Listen carefully and take heed of the advice your hearing so it doesn't come back to hurt you.

_____

_____

_____

_____

_____

_____

Many don't understand the mental and physical toll a divorce and custody battle have on someone. A divorce is physically draining, but issues dealing with Parental Alienation sucks all of your hope out of you and leads you to a point of wanting to give up on life. As I was thinking about this, I was reminded of what Winston Churchill had to face during the dark days of World War II.

On May 10, 1940, Churchill was elected as the Prime Minister of England. The timing was exquisitely important as much of Europe was being taken over by Nazi Germany and Adolf Hitler. Nearly 400,000 British and French troops surrounded at Dunkirk on the French coast narrowly escaped by evacuating to Britain. As Luftwaffe planes started bombing England during the Battle of Britain, the country was on the verge of losing hope.

Great Britain was at a turning point and required a strong leader to rally the populace and beat back the enemy. Churchill's first speech as Prime Minster took the country by surprise. After telling the English public that he had nothing to offer but blood, toil, tears, and sweat, he urged everyone in the sound of his voice to fight Nazi tyranny on the seas, in the air, on the landing grounds, in the fields, and in the streets, should Hitler's soldiers invade their island. They could never surrender.

Churchill raised British spirits at a time when many thought all hope of holding back the Nazi armies was lost. By the fall of 1941, more than a year later, the tide had turned, but Churchill recognized there was much sacrifice and danger ahead. He addressed the British public on October 29, 1941, and urged them to stay the course and never give in to Nazi tyranny because he knew there were many key battles ahead. Less than three years later, England would be the launching point of the greatest sea-borne invasion in history when 6,000 landing craft carrying 176,000 troops landed on the beaches of Normandy.

The irony was Sir Winston Churchill was replaced by the voters just two months after defeating Hitler and his regime in 1945. But complacency and political turmoil led to Churchill's reelection six years later in 1951, showing that it's never too late to stage a comeback.

The reason I'm sharing Churchill's story is because the hardest part of Parental Alienation is not losing hope. I can tell you that just like Winston Churchill, I felt the forces were stacked up against me and my world was caving in. I have heard on many occasions that my story is unbelievable and that I must be lying as to how a loving parent could be deprived of a relationship with his children unless he did something greatly wrong. They agree with me that the courts would ever do that, but they did. The truth is the courts eliminate parental rights or create for an environment for parental alienation in almost every custody case. Unless you've been through this like I have, you would never know it.

Upon my divorce, and the rumors from my ex, many of those who called themselves friends abandoned me. Today, I have only two people in my life who have known me and my kids before my divorce. I have been demoralized by being homeless. For six months, I slept on an air mattress at my friend's office at night and bathed out of a bucket with a washcloth as I did not have a place to shower. I lived out of my car during the day or spent my waking hours at the local coffee shop because I was unable to get a job. And on top of this, I was fighting in every way to be a part of the lives of my children.

I had only two choices at the time: either forge ahead or just give up on life. Each time I thought it would be easier to give up, I was drawn back to those four children that God had entrusted to me and the promises He gave me for them. It was those promises that inspired me to "never give in" and fight be a part of my children's lives.

Exercise #2:

Turning toward your issues, have you ever felt that the battle is far bigger than you? Are you fighting in a way so that you don't lose hope? If so, describe what you're doing to not lose hope.

_____

_____

_____

_____

_____

In 1940, the British needed someone to breath hope into their county and found that in Winston Churchill. It's important to find a small circle of friends who can breathe life and hope into your situation. Who is the person encouraging you? What is he or she doing to breathe hope back into you? Are you able to encourage yourself and see hope when others cannot be there? Are you able to press in to God during this dark time?

_____

_____

_____

_____

_____

_____

Sometimes after defeating an adversary, you can't become apathetic or complacent of your condition or look for a new mate to fill a void since that may create a new set of problems and force you to start over again. Is there anything within your fight that is making you apathetic? Or are you looking to someone else to help you resolve your issues? List some of those things that may be a distraction or cause apathy or complacency in your healing process or rob you of hope.

_____

_____

_____

_____

_____

_____

One of the biggest battles for someone dealing with Parental Alienation is the ongoing financial battle. There are many things that take a financial toll on a parent dealing with a divorce and custody issues: child support, court costs, attorney fees, time away from work, and your living costs. Then there are other expenses mandated by the state.

The court costs and attorney fees are one thing, but child support can be extremely complicated, especially when two states are involved. The laws vary from state to state and year by year, and some states change the rules during your court-ordered support period. Most states mandate that a paying parent must support minor children until they emancipate at the age of eighteen, while others, like New York, mandate that a paying parent is to pay child support until children are twenty-four, if they are still in school.

The goal of the state regarding child support is to keep the paying parent in arrears even after a child emancipates with additional fees, interest, or incorrect records. There are many theories why this occurs, which I will not get into, but I will share some of the financial toll I was subjected to.

The premise of the battle my ex had with me was to make sure she maximized her share of support. The state of original jurisdiction, at the time, was structured to where child support was based on the amount of visitation, or shared parenting time, one had with the children. The closer to a 50/50 split, the closer to zero the obligation of support was. The less time one parent had with their children, the greater the obligation of support was, which was based on the combined incomes, after taxes, by both parents, and not to exceed 50 percent of one parent's total income.

The state where my ex moved to was different. In that state, child support ~~as it~~ was based on a percentage per child of the obligating parent's income, up to 50 percent. When the dissolution of our marriage was completed in that state, the judge based the child support on 80/20 visitation, meaning I would have to pay 80 percent of the support because I was only given an assumed amount of 20 percent of visitation. The way the courts look at things, the less time you spend with your children, the more you owe because the other parent assumes a greater financial burden. The parent who spends the most time with the children gets more compensation for her (or his) time. Additionally, this amount could not be written off in taxes, and I was not given the child tax credit, which is typical in most states.

The goal of my ex-wife, however, was to make sure I would pay 100 percent of the child support obligation by removing *any* visitation between me and my children to maximize her benefit. The issue she had was the judge in the state of origin would not hear her request because he knew what her goal was. The only way she could obtain her wishes was to get a reconsideration of my parental rights in another state then take that order back for a modification of support. Her greatest risk was that the state of origin would eventually change its calculations of support to be the same as the state she moved the children to, which, in turn, would not give her more money but would ruin my relationship with my children.

If this weren't bad enough, I had to deal with two states that refused to communicate with each other and kept conflicting records. If I wasn't in court for matters of custody, I was in court on matters of child support. In some cases, I had to sue the state to get our records reconciled.

All the legal maneuverings took a toll on me financially, but there was another factor that I hadn't considered. Due to the amount of time I had to take off traveling to court, writing documents, or dealing with attorneys, I lost several jobs. It took me nearly seven years to get a job that paid me a decent wage only to lose that one because I had to leave work to travel every six weeks or so across the country and make another court appearance. My ex-wife thought of every little thing she could to drag me into court, filing one frivolous motion after another. When I lost that job, I started freelancing to have the flexibility needed to defend myself in court, but my earnings were greatly diminished.

The financial battle is just as real as the custody and visitation battle. The reality of what was going on was summed up by what ex-wife said in a few words: "I want to destroy you." Unfortunately, an alienating parent's ultimate goal is to erase the very existence of the other parent.

Exercise #3:

Knowing that your back is up against the wall, financially, what steps can you take to stabilize your situation and put yourself on track to handle your finances and obligations?

_____

_____

_____

_____

_____

_____

_____

_____

- What are some steps you can take to help alleviate the financial stress? This may require you doing a budget and sticking with it or cooking and preparing your own meals.

_____

_____

_____

_____

_____

- As you look to the future, what are some things you may want to do with or for your children?

_____

_____

_____

_____

_____

Challenge:

Pastor Derwin Gray of Transformation Church in Indian Land, South Carolina, did a sermon series called "Hope Dealers." Pastor Gray talked about how one can go from receiving hope to becoming a "hope dealer" to others.

This is my challenge to you and something I challenged myself with: in the midst of my pain, when I thought all hope was lost of ever seeing my kids again or having a great relationship with them. I decided to step out in faith and reflect God's hope to others.

Seek God's goodness in this journey and being able to serve others. This will require you to be intentional in what you do and may require you to start with baby steps.

If you're still in the battle and needing hope, though, I encourage you to find someone who can breathe hope back into you. It may be necessary to get counseling and find a support group.

Another thing you can do is read Ephesians 6:10-20 and pay close attention to verse 18 from The Message. I'm adding my thoughts in the brackets:

> "In the same way, prayer is essential in this ongoing warfare [journey]. Pray hard and long. Pray for your brothers and sisters [those that are in the same fight]. Keep your eyes open. Keep each other's spirits up so no one falls behind or drops out."

Prayer:

I like this excerpt from the Sermon on the Mount from Matthew 6:9-13 (MSG):

> "Our Father in heaven,
> Reveal who You are.
> Set the world right;
> Do what is best—
> > as above, so below.
> Keep us alive with three square meals.

Keep us forgiven with you and forgiving others.
Keep us safe from ourselves and the Devil.
You're in charge!
You can do anything you want!
You're ablaze with beauty!
Yes, Yes. Yes.

Additional Scriptures to dwell on throughout the week:

- Zephaniah 3:17 talks about how the Lord is in your presence.
- Isaiah 40:31 reminds us that God will renew your strength.
- Ephesians 6:10-20 is all about the armor of God.

Continue to put on the armor of God each day. Pray the Lord's Prayer and examine it in a way that will help you apply it to your life and journey.

Journal:

Take some time to journal your thoughts on what you've read so far and strategies that would be helpful to implement:

_____

_____

_____

_____

_____

_____

_____

3 The Effects of Parental Alienation on the Extended Family

"Resentment is like taking poison and waiting for the other person die."
—Malachy McCourt, Irish-American actor

I can't tell you the number of social science experts who say that divorce doesn't have an adverse effect on the extended family. That declaration can't be further from the truth. The next time I read something like that, I'd like to tell the researchers, "Try living in my shoes for a day."

As I dived into this topic and talked to estranged parents, I spotted a pattern. As one person from one of my Parental Alienation groups stated, "The divorce of my daughter and separation from my grandchildren have torn up our family." I heard similar comments from my family, and I was reminded continuously by my parents what the toll of my broken family has been like for them.

For example, a few years back, my parents were looking forward to celebrating their fiftieth wedding anniversary and really wanted my children to be there. When my ex-wife got wind of that, she made sure that wasn't going to happen and did her best to stop any communication between my children and their grandparents.

I asked a judge to step in and have my ex bring the children to my parents' home, which was in another state, so they could be part of the fiftieth wedding anniversary and see my side of the family, as well as me. The judge, however, refused my request for reasons I do not know. Once again, we lost an invaluable opportunity for my children to take part in an important family event and get to know their relatives better.

There are many ways in which the extended family can be stopped from communicating with the children or simply erased from their lives.

This can range from being blocked from cell phones, email addresses being changed, or being "unfriended" on social media platforms like Facebook or Instagram. An ex can move to another address and fail to give the new address in a timely manner, or even at all, which means that cards and gifts may never arrive at their new home. There are even times where the alienating parent will even withhold gifts and letters or have them returned so they can play the victim card to the children and paint the absent parent and his family in a bad light.

These examples of Parental Alienation are real and common. Traci L. Slatton, an author and columnist for the Huffington Post website, addressed how parental alienation and inference works to affect both the targeted parent as well as his extended family. Slatton described the process as a form of brainwashing or manipulation of children's minds with the goal of convincing them that their feelings and thoughts about their family members are contrived or need to be discarded. "Children fall prey to the alienating parent's tactics as a means of escaping conflict," she wrote, and she's right—children *hate* conflict, especially between warring parents.

From my experience, children are stripped of their feelings and often manipulated to say something or do something outlandish against the alienated parent. It comes with the territory.

I'll never forget a Skype call with my daughter, fourteen at the time. This was a court-ordered phone call, meaning that I had to go to a judge and tell him that my ex was keeping me from speaking to my children. When the Skype call began, I could tell that my daughter felt like she was under extreme pressure speaking with me, so I shouldn't have been surprised when she lashed out like I was her piñata for the day.

"Why are you at Starbucks?" she asked. "You're always there."

She could tell from the background that I was making the Skype call from a Starbucks, which is what I had to do since I couldn't afford wi-fi at home. I was a bit taken aback, but I kept my cool.

"Is that a problem?" I had on earphones so nobody else could hear her.

"Yes, it sure is!"

"Why is that?"

"I'm mad because you're spending all this money on coffee rather than paying child support like you're supposed to."

Now I was getting it. She was hearing a load of BS from my ex about how I wasn't paying child support when, in fact, I was current. I tried a different tack.

"How much do you think I spend on coffee?" I inquired.

My daughter was ready with a figure. "You spend $2,786 per year," she said.

Where she got that figure, I didn't know, but I didn't spend anything like that on Starbucks drinks in a year.

I mentioned the exchange to a judge a couple months later in a general discussion about how my ex was saying things to my kids that either weren't true or shouldn't be said about me.

"I take great issue with what your daughter said about the coffee shop and the defendant," the judge began, addressing my ex-wife. "There is no child who could come up with something like that. Furthermore, I take issue with children talking to their father with such great disrespect and the demand that he incriminates himself for abusing them. Even in cases where I know that children have been abused, those children do not talk in such a way as these children have of their father. I cannot help but feel that they are being influenced by someone else. If it's not their mother, then it would have to be the counselor the mother is having them see."

What happened next surprised me even more. Rachel's attorney, a woman, stood up and blamed my daughter for being an evil and manipulating person. Talk about throwing my fourteen-year-old daughter under the bus!

A couple years later, I found out that the alienation broadened beyond me to my extended family. You see, my kids reside within an hour of four of their cousins and two aunts and uncles, yet none of them had spent any time with them. Even worse was when I talked to my niece, their oldest cousin, I was told that my ex had made the rounds, calling different family members and telling them that if they even attempted to contact my children, then she would cut them off by blocking their numbers. This kind of thing has been going on for years.

That's why I feel strongly that alienation is way bigger than just a single spouse like myself. Over time, I found that my ex's actions impacted my nieces and nephews as well, especially those who lived closest to them.

They'd ask me multiple questions about my kids—like how they were doing, if there was anything happening with the courts, or when I expected to see them next.

One of my brothers mentioned an incident he had with his preschool-age daughter. He told me that he went to the basement and saw a picture of my kids that his daughter had put up in her play area.

"Dad, I like those kids," she said in an innocent voice. Yet because of my ex's actions, she would never get to know my children—or even have pictures of my kids when they were older.

With all the chaos and separation, I'm reminded that the greatest things a child wants is the stability and freedom to love their family in a healthy way.

Part 1:

Have you ever taken the time to look at how the alienation has affected your extended family?

Begin by reading Deuteronomy 5:8-10 (MSG):

> "No carved gods of any size, shape or form whatsoever, whether of things that fly or walk or swim. Don't bow down to them and don't serve the because I am God, your God, and I'm a most jealous God. I hold parents responsible for any sins they pass on to their children to the third generation, and yes even to the fourth generation. But I'm lovingly loyal to the thousands who love me and keep My commandments."

According to this passage from Deuteronomy, God warns that worshipping other gods effects many generations, up to even the fourth generation. Although you may not have carved idols made of wood or stone inside your house, there could be other idols in your life or the life of your ex. I'm thinking of the pursuit of money, drinking alcohol, wearing fashionable clothes, driving fast cars, or following your favorite NFL team. When your focus is taken off the Creator and placed on the created, it stunts your spiritual growth and skews your perspective of what God's promise is for your life.

Exercises:

- In terms of the "bigger picture," how would you define your family—post separation or divorce? What are your expectations for your children if you could sum them up in a couple of sentences?

___

- Looking back a few generations, what things have impacted you to make you into the person you are today, both good and bad?

___

- What goals and dreams did you have for your kids before the divorce or separation? Write down the things that have been fulfilled and unfulfilled. Which list is longer?

_____

_____

_____

_____

_____

_____

- Time to get real: How has your separation/divorce/ impacted your extended family? Have you taken the time to ask your parents, siblings, or other family members how they feel about not having a relationship with your children? Ask them if they're able to talk to them or send them cards and gifts.

_____

_____

_____

_____

_____

_____

- Now would be a good time to question how you view your children. Do you see them as an entrusted gift from God, even though you no longer live together?

_____

_____

_____

_____

_____

Although separation from your children can have a toxic effect on them for many years, your reaction to how things are can have as equally a negative effect on them as well.

One thing I needed to do was to take a unique perspective on "who" my kids are. Since we didn't live together any longer, I needed to look at them in a different light. What I mean is that it was easy to look at my children as a possession rather than an entrusted gift from God. I think that's because I was so focused on exercising my parental rights.

Part 2:

Let's explore the idea of looking at our children as a possession or a blessing. Read Job 1:21-22 (MSG):

> Naked I came from my mother's womb, naked I will return to the womb of the earth. God gives, God takes. God's name be ever blessed. Not once through all of this did Job sin; not once did he blame God.

This verse may not seem to address how parents should look at their

Ex's & Oh's

kids, but the important phrase is that God gives and takes—meaning good stuff and bad stuff happens—but His name is forever to be blessed. The important idea to keep in mind that you are entrusted with everything you have and have been given.

When you understand how to properly manage what you have been given, you can savor the blessings God has given you and better understand how to have faith deep enough to resolve the issues at hand.

If you were to read more about Job in the Old Testament, you will find that he was a man who had everything—money, family, property, and thousands of animals, but with the snap of a finger, he lost everything, including his health, family, and material belongings.

These setbacks tested his faith in God. The Book of Job is about his unwavering faith, even though I'm not saying all the horrible diseases and loss of family and wealth didn't affect him emotionally. Nonetheless, God blessed Job in abundance for his faith and faithfulness.

It's easy to feel angry, violated, and abused when something is taken away, but when children are removed from your life—either through divorce or death—it changes you forever. The heavy impact takes you away from a proper perspective of God.

I feel like there are two perspectives to consider. The first is called the horizontal perspective, which is where all you can see is what is in front of you. The other is the vertical perspective, which allows you to see things from above while allowing a broader perspective of everything going on around you.

- What is your perspective? Are you the only looking at things head on, or are you able to see things from a higher elevation so that you can have a broader perspective? Give three ways you may see things from a horizontal perspective, and write down three ways you may be seeing things from a vertical perspective regarding your children.

_____

_____

_____

- Have you spoken with your extended family about any of the alienation issues that I've been describing? What's their perspective? Do they feel the same pain that you do from the separation from your children?

- When I changed my perspective from this being about "MY CHILDREN" to "GOD CHOSE ME TO BE A PARENT FOR MY CHILDREN," I was able to take a vertical perspective of God's promise, which reaches beyond my children for generations to bring glory to God in a different way.

    Do you feel that God has spoken promises to you about your children? If so, list them here.

Challenge:

For the longest time, I had such a problem with the impact of my divorce and separation from my kids as well as the effect it had on my parents, siblings, and other extended family because my pain was so great. When I heard my mother talk about her struggles that she'd had with my marital breakup and loss of the kids, I became upset and defensive. What I couldn't understand right away was just how those actions had consequences and had repercussions on more people than I thought.

For some time, God has been talking to me about standing stones. What I mean is too often we look at stones as rigid, hard, and painful, but the reality is that many times they are there to remind us of the tough times God delivered us from.

Our lives are meant to be standing stones to remind our children and grandchildren of the things God has delivered us from so His promises are fulfilled for His glory and future generations.

So, let me ask you this: What kind of legacy are you leaving your children? What do they see in you when you're together? Do you want them to have a reflection of the suffering you had to live with, or are you willing to change course and make a difference in your children?

When you look at your children as a promise rather than a possession, as well your situation from a different perspective, you can start a new course. It's important to lay the correct groundwork so they can see the epic beauty and promise that is meant for them. Sure, you may have made mistakes in life, but it's never too late to make a difference in the lives of your children. God can change their perspective and change the course of the damage that has been done if you are willing to have a vertical perspective and put in the work.

Prayer:

Lord God, make us a standing stone for generations to come. May our children and grandchildren look past the sins, brokenness, and pain we may have had and let them see Your goodness and the faith you gave us to break the chains that have held us down. May we see our children as a promise for your greater plans in life rather than a possession. Regardless what happens in our relationships, may we trust You like Job and see your goodness in all You do. In Jesus' name, amen.

Additional Scriptures to dwell on throughout the week:

- Joshua 3 and 4
- Job 1
- Jerimiah 29 and 33

Journal:

4 Loving Your Child from a Distance

"The scariest thing about distance is you don't whether they'll miss you or forget you."
—Nicholas Sparks, author of *The Notebook*

Being a parent is a journey into uncharted territory, but being a non-custodial parent is like being blindfolded and being thrown down a mineshaft with your hands tied behind your back. If you're a non-custodial parent or grandparent who's in a situation where the other party is beyond unreasonable, you may be asking; "Is it possible to be an example and still parent my child through this mess?"

The answer is yes, but only to a degree. The future will require you to be even more sacrificial and understanding than when you were active in their lives. The future will require you to put aside you dreams and goals for a long time.

In the meantime, you can continue to love your children from a distance. You can transcend the bitterness and hurt caused to you by another adult who may be using the children to deliberately hurt you. You may be asking, *How do I do this? What does this even look like?*

I know too well what it's been like to be baffled by this mystery. I thought loving from a distance was just the thousand miles after their mother moved them to another state, but it was far more than that once the games began and the court cases and accusations became endless. Everyone would tell me to just keep loving my kids from a distance, yet no one was able to explain what that looked like.

Although in my personal case, *Loving your children from a distance*

Ex's & Oh's

meant thousands of miles of separation, the reality has been this: being cut off from my kids due to a court order restricting access created a chasm as large as the physical distance. Even if your kids are living next door, a judicial order can make you feel like they're halfway across the country.

What many don't understand is where the chasm comes from. The truth is that's it's more than the miles, a court order, or not having the resources to be there for your children. I say that because the reality is that the separation caused a loss of your identity.

When a couple splits up and divorces, many counselors and family psychologists refer to the situation as needing to "find your new norm." Similarly, the same type of thing happens with parenting, but the difference is that custodial and non-custodial parents are often distracted by everything going on around them, causing them not to be as effective parents as they should be.

As a result, they lose or sacrifice their identity as a parent but for different reasons. A custodial parent may be too occupied drawing battle lines against the other parent and giving into the whims of their children so she can earn their loyalty. In contrast, a non-custodial parent may attempt to relinquish his role as a parent and become a friend or a peer to their children when he spends quality time with them. As a result, both parents lose their parental identity. Children pick up on that and take advantage of the situation by acting out, when what they really want is a stable family life and establishing their own identity.

Here's an example of what I mean. During my separation, my estranged wife wanted to go with me and my children to the mall to shop for Easter clothes for the kids. I was with the boys, and she decided to take my daughter into a designer boutique. When I met the two of them at the designer store, the next thing I knew I was being set up by the two of them.

My daughter saw a dress that was about $250 and asked me if I would buy it for her. I told her no because I did not have that kind of money. The next thing I knew, I was given attitude by my daughter, claiming that us being separated should make for more things for her to have. What I did not expect was being painted as enemy number one by her mother. She told my daughter that it was okay that I said she couldn't have the dress because I, as her father, was just being selfish. The seeds were planted of just how my ex would portray me in the future and the battles I would face with my kids.

Remind yourself that once a parent, always a parent, no matter how close or how far you live from your children. Children will look to be the equal to both parents in order to get a semblance of stability. The key is you must understand that your role is to be their parent and know when to say yes and not be afraid to say no.

God gave you a role as a father or mother when your children were born, through birth or adoption, and no one can take that away from you, not even a court.

When I think about this concept, I cannot help but reflect on one of the most common verses used at weddings:

> Therefore what God has joined together, let not man separate.
> —Mark 10:9 (NKJV)

Now I'd like you to read this verse:
"For You formed my inward parts;
You covered me in my mother's womb.
I will praise You, for I am fearfully and wonderfully made;
Marvelous are Your works.
And that my soul knows very well."
—Psalm 139:13-14 (NKJV)

The very foundation of being a parent is something that God formed on two separate but equal levels as He knitted the very parts of your children in the womb and joined your role as a parent that was never meant to be separated. God gave you your children for two specific purposes:

1. As a blessing to you.
2. To mirror what He made in the Garden of Eden in order to draw you into a personal relationship with Him.

Once you understand that loving your children isn't a chore or a chance to manipulate to get something in return, but rather as an opportunity to woo their hearts into relationship with you just like God woos you to Him, then you'll see your kids in a different light. So, if God doesn't draw you back to Him through manipulation or bullying or making you think in a certain way, why should a parent not also act in a way to their kids as God does to us and woo their hearts into relationship with you as his parent?

Part 1:

Let's look at what "loving from a distance" really means, starting with Ephesians 6:4 (MSG):

> "Father [parent/grandparent], don't exasperate your children by coming down hard on them . . ."

> The New King James version says, "Don't provoke your children to wrath."

When my children were little, I gave them each a nickname. For many years, they wore those names with great pride and answered to them. It wasn't until my divorce that the kids did a 180 and took great offense to those names. To get back at me, they started calling me by my first name rather than "Dad." I'll admit that stung.

I had to back off, though, on something that was acceptable at one time because they objected to my terms of endearment, even though I considered it petty and immature. For all I knew, their mother instructed them to address me that way. Nonetheless, I had to respect their wishes because I didn't know the full story and was aware that they weren't able to process their pain from the past.

Maybe you've had the same experience. If so, here are some things you will need to ask yourself.

- Are you mad about the circumstances you are in with your limited role as a parent with your children? If so, what is making you angry?

___

- Are you taking a different approach when you have a conversation with your kids? Are you touching any "hot buttons" with them? I had to learn not to call them by their nicknames or bring up certain subjects. Do you have a similar story to tell? If so, list some of the areas of conflict you may be experiencing with your kids and how you can resolve them.

___

- Do you know your children well enough to divert them from anger? How are you navigating these sorts of conversations with them?

- Are you able to show them how to think differently about you in certain situations, which will create a healthy environment in the future and help them want to spend more time with you? When you're together, do you show them that they are more important than your cell phone, appointments, or anything else they may misinterpret? How are you showing them that they are important to your life?

Keep in mind that the goal is not to criticize your children, the other parent, or their friends. If you find it necessary to comment about any of these areas, make sure it is not in a condescending way, but rather in an instructional way to allow them to think. Ask open-ended questions, including how they think God would think of the situation.

Part 2:

At the beginning of this chapter, I shared a quote from Nicolas Sparks, the author of *The Notebook*, about how the scariest thing about distance is that you don't know whether they'll miss you or forget you. Regarding this quote, think about how distance effects your relationship with your kids, creating a chasm between you and your children.

- What is your greatest fear in your relationship—being limited in contact or even eliminated between you and your children?

_____

- How can you make the best of the time you have with your children? What steps are you taking to make those times impressionable rather than marginalized and forgotten?

_____

_____

_____

_____

So often in divorce with children, a non-custodial parent can feel as if he is being used like a rag and forgotten. That's usually not forever, though. I've spoken to parents who told me that once their children hit about the age of twenty-five, they often came around when they went through a major life event or trauma of their own. It may be a marriage, having a child, a divorce, or needing money for a personal venture. Now that you've heard this concept, what can you do to prepare for these milestones in your children's lives?

_____

_____

_____

_____

_____

Part 3:

Consider this second part of Ephesians 6:4 (MSG):

> ". . . take them by the hand and lead them in the way of the Master."

When it comes to guiding your children, this may be one of the hardest areas to deal with. You may be asking, *How can I lead my children when my time with them is so limited?*

This is going to take a little more creativity, careful thought, and a lot of prayer. Remember who the first Father was—God. He showed us what marriage and family was by how He instructed, provided provision, and gave consequences for bad decisions. Look at what the Psalmist had to say.

> A refusal to correct is a refusal to love;
>   love your children by disciplining them.
>   —Proverbs 13:24 (MSG)

Remember, you're still your children's parent, regardless of the distance or frequency of spending time with them. Stay the course of training your children about right and wrong but in a loving way that will be accepted by them. Live by example when you can.

Below are some questions you will need to reconcile with.

1. Are you treating you children like you are their parent or more like their friend? If the latter, why do you feel you have to parent in that way?

_____

_____

_____

_____

_____

_____

_____

_____

2. How are you leading your children to the Master? Are you submitting your will, thoughts, and actions to God daily? Are you in the Word consistently to find out where God is leading you?

_____

_____

_____

_____

_____

_____

_____

3. What activities are you involved with that can be an example to your children? What activities can help you learn how to be the best parent for them?

_____

_____

_____

_____

_____

_____

_____

Challenge:

Trying to lead can be very difficult, especially when God has entrusted you with the task. One person left with this charge was Joshua from the Old Testament.

Joshua told each of the twelve tribes of Israel that he wanted them to send one person to grab a large stone from the middle of the Jordan River as a reminder of God's goodness. Here is the applicable Scripture:

> And Joshua said to them, "Pass on before the ark of the Lord your God into the midst of the Jordan, and take up each of you a stone upon his shoulder, according to the number of the tribes of the people of Israel, that this may be a sign among you. When your children ask in time to come, 'What do those stones mean to you?' then you shall tell them that the waters of the Jordan were cut off before the ark of the covenant of the Lord. When it passed over the Jordan, the waters of the Jordan were cut off. So, these stones shall be to the people of Israel a memorial forever."
> —Joshua 4:5-7 (ESV)

To most, what happened may seem odd, but God knew that the generations needed to remember what God has done for them.

As you walk this journey of parenting, likely as a parent separated from his children, you must remember that with each step, you're creating a stone memorial for your children to look back on. If you proceed according to godly principles, those stones will have great significance for many generations to come and contribute to their success.

You and your children can stop the raging waters when you're willing to set up the standing stones for your family. Remember you are doing this for your children today and your grandchildren tomorrow.

Prayer:

Lord God, search my heart and allow my thoughts to be more in line with yours. Don't allow bitterness to gain a foothold during this battle or time of loneliness. Allow me to find joy in the journey and seek You in all decisions. Allow me to be the best parent and grandparent my children need me to be regardless of the miles and frequency during this time. Father God, I ask that You grant restoration according to Your Word and healing in my life, so I may see the bigger picture and be part of Your larger plan. Forgive me for any thoughts, words, or actions I may have had during this time. In Christ's name, amen.

Additional Scriptures to dwell on throughout the week:

Colossians 3:21: *Be careful not to crush your child's spirit.*
Ephesians 4:31: *Let go of bitterness.*
Proverbs 22:6: *Train up a child.*
Joshua 24:15: *As for me and my house, we will serve the Lord.*
Jeremiah 29:11: *I have plans for you that will blow your mind.*

Journal:

_____

_____

_____

_____

_____

_____

_____

5

What Did You Say?

> "Most people do not listen with the intent to understand; they listen with the intent to reply."
> —Stephen R. Covey, author of *The 7 Habits of Highly Effective People*

Everyone knows that children say the funniest things.

Being a father of four children, I have held fast to the humorous and quirky things my kids have said in the past. One of the best things I was left with after the divorce were the simple memories and delightful impressions my children made on my life.

When my youngest son was little, he had a saying when he was confused. He'd speak in his raspy voice and ask me, "What did you say?" I can still hear him saying that in my mind.

I keep coming back to that very question, with a smile, when I started writing this chapter.

Listening to your children's thoughts and feelings during the turbulent time of post-divorce is one of the most important things you can do. I certainly understand that it's easy to get caught up with the legal issues and what the other parent is saying or doing against you and your extended family, but if you keep asking, "What did you say?", then you'll really hear their heart and pain in the situation.

Your kids are carrying around pain as equally as you are. They do not have the capability of processing what's happening to them like adults do. What children are looking for is stability in their lives at a time when they know their lives reside on a fault line called divorce. What sets off this fault line more frequently than anything else is when a parent puts the child in the middle of a tug-of-war or, even worse, when each parent is so absorbed by his pain and rights that he does not realize the adverse effects he's having on his children.

Scripture gives us guidelines to assure the safety of our children and family. The Book of Ephesians calls us not to exasperate our children or come down hard on them, which can crush their spirits. You should listen with the intent of understanding someone's perspective rather than with the intent of replying with your next point. Too often human nature, especially in a heated discussion or arguments, lacks understanding because we're wrapped up in our emotions.

Part 1:

How are your words to your children? Read 1 Corinthians 13:1-3 from The Message below:

> "If I speak with human eloquence and angelic ecstasy but don't love, I'm nothing but the creaking of a rusty gate. If I speak God's Word with power, revealing all his mysteries and making everything plain as day, and if I have faith that says to a mountain 'Jump' and it jumps, but I don't have love, I'm nothing. If I give everything I own to the poor and even go to the stake to be burned as a martyr, I've gotten nowhere. So, no matter what I say, what I believe, and what I do, I'm bankrupt without love."

- After reading this passage from 1 Corinthians, what do you think your children are seeing in you and your life? Do your kids see you as an effective person for God's plan in their lives, or do they view you as a hypocrite? Write down some things your children may have said about you post-divorce.

_____

_____

- If your children are saying negative things about you after the divorce but previously looked at you as their hero with admiration, how do you refute their claims? Note: It is typical for children to demonize one parent over another following an ugly divorce or a marital split riddled with parental interference.

- If your children see you in a bad light, name some non-manipulative steps you are taking so that your children can see a different side of you. This can be achieved through counseling, getting plugged into a church or support group, or finding an accountability partner of the same sex to confide in.

J.K. Nation

_____

_____

_____

It's easy to beat up yourself because of what your children say about you or your character. If this is how you're feeling, take this as an opportunity to listen to a different perspective of who you are and how others may see you. I'm not saying what is being said of you is true, only that there may be some validity that you can use to refine your character to become a better reflection of yourself. Prayerfully ask God to show you these areas that need improvement.

Part 2:

What is your child saying? Read Job 13:13-17 (NLT):

> "Be silent now and leave me alone, that I may speak—and I am willing to face the consequences. Yes, I will take my life into my own hand and say what I really think. God may kill me for saying this—in fact, I expect him to. Nevertheless, I am going to argue my case with him. This at least will be in my favor, that I am not godless, to be rejected instantly from his presence. Listen closely to what I am about to say. Hear me out."

Listening may be one of the most difficult things to do because it requires you to be quiet and to hear something that may not be that pleasant. Likewise, in any relationship, you we must be able to listen and listen well if you desire a healthy relationship.

This is true whether it is with your ex-spouse, current spouse or girlfriend, family member, fellow employee, or neighbor. Moreover, if you expect your children to feel validated and respected, you must be able to listen to their hearts. This does not necessarily mean that you must agree with their statements or requests, but you do have to listen.

One of the most difficult things we have, as a society, is understanding the difference between respect and honor and being able to differentiate it with our children. Although our English language uses the terms *respect* and *honor* synonymously for each other, they do have different implications. This is where listening for understanding verses listening to get your point across comes into play.

In order to listen better to understand, you must know the difference between honor and respect. Honor means to treat someone with admiration, while respect refers to a *feeling* of admiration that is given to someone. When I found this out, it made a world of difference with what I heard my children saying to me and what I wanted to get across to them.

One thing my daughter would always say to me was, "You don't respect us," and in turn, she would dishonor me as her father and show disrespect. What my daughter was basically saying was she had no regard to the position I held as her father, so because she did not respect me, she wasn't going to honor me.

Not only that, but she expected her position as my child to be valued equal to my role as her father. As a parent, it was difficult if not impossible for me to elevate her position as a child to that of me, as her parent, even though I valued what she said and who she was as an individual.

To bring things around full circle, let me share the following quote from business author Stephen Covey again:

> "Most people do not listen with the intent to understand; they listen with the intent to reply."

- Which type of listener are you? Give some methods you can use to be a better listener and resolve conflict.

_____

_____

_____

- Have you taken the time, since your divorce, to talk to your children and see what they have to say, think, and feel? Some of their feelings may be about your divorce, you, your ex-spouse, their living arrangements, or even just what is making them sad and confused. List four questions that you can ask your children—questions that will allow them to open their hearts.

- Children feel they need to be respected. (This does not mean that you are their equal or peer, however. You are still the parent.) Write down in a couple sentences how you feel you show respect to your children.

- Have you ever found yourself asking the question "What did you say?" to God? Do you feel that perhaps God hasn't listened to you and your heart? List some of those ways in which you feel that God has not heard your heart.

_____

_____

_____

_____

_____

_____

Challenge:

Listening to the hearts of your children is important, especially during times of turmoil and tragedy. Whether it is a divorce, death, or a major change in address, it's always important to hear the hearts of your children. Sure, there are times where you feel that it's important to give advice to them, but it may be more important to allow your children to speak without you saying a word and being a good listener.

When you are with your children, try something a little different in your communication pattern by performing this exercise. You will need a ping pong paddle and a timer (a digital version on a smartphone works well but a sand timer may work best). If you have older children, they may think this exercise is a little corny or impractical, but it's all about how you present it and your attitude during the activity.

You will need to sit in a comfortable setting, preferably either at the kitchen table or in family room on different sofas or chairs. Whoever has the paddle has the floor to speak freely and honestly about whatever they wish during the time. No one can respond to what was said unless it is a direct question. If you respond, avoid making excuses or blaming someone else another for what was stated. It's always best to evaluate what is said and take responsibility, asking forgiveness when necessary. Refrain from anger or blaming the other parent for anything, no matter how difficult.

A suggested time frame for each person to speak should be between three and five minutes. This exercise gives you the tools to communicate better and express your feelings. The exercise also teaches children how to listen.

Prayer:

Lord God, please allow me to be slow to speak so I may listen. Show me how best to hear the heart of my children. Teach me to listen with understanding. In Christ's name, amen.

Additional Scriptures to dwell on throughout the week:

James 3:8-12: Can the tongue bring forth blessings and curses at the same time?

James 1:19: Be quick to listen but slow to anger.

Ephesians 4:26: Do not let the sun go down upon your wrath.

Psalm 56:8: God counts your tears and keeps track of your restless nights.

Take a look at Job's journey. He lost everything, yet because he endured God restored to him everything in greater abundance.

Journal:

_____

_____

_____

_____

6

How Do I Deal with the Pain and Heal Properly?

> "A successful man is one who can lay a firm foundation with the bricks others have thrown at him."
>
> —David Brinkley, American newscaster for ABC and NBC

Divorce can be one of the greatest pains ever, especially if one has been cheated on. What can be even worse though, in a divorce, is when one person decides to use the children as weapons by convincing them to withdraw their love of the alienated parent and poison their thinking to the degree that the alienated parent is viewed as a bad person in the minds of the children.

This leaves children feeling unloved and confused and the alienated parent feeling frustrated as well as violated—because he feels like he has been kicked out of his children's lives. Having lived through this, I can honestly and soberly say that the act of alienation contributes to feelings of low self-esteem, fatigue, anxiety, depression, and anger. Unfortunately, I've even heard that in some cases of PA, parents have committed suicide because they were left with no hope for their futures.

Children experience their own set of feelings, but their greatest ones are abandonment and instability. In one conversation with my children, I gleaned from them that because I was dating someone with kids of her own, they felt like they were being rejected and replaced by me, which solidified (in their minds) their sense of rejection. As a result, it was their turn to deal with feelings of instability, anger, depression, and anxiety.

Many studies show that children of divorce have a higher rate of low self-esteem, a harder time concentrating, a greater rate of suicide, more instances of teen pregnancy, a higher risk of cutting, and divorcing when they become adults. They struggle to have meaningful relationships at a rate of up to 60 percent, according to statistics from Focus on the Family and WebMD.

So, following that preamble, what is the key to dealing with the pain of divorce and healing properly?

There are no easy answers because circumstances vary drastically. It's impossible to compare what happened in your relationship that led to your divorce with what happened to my marriage, but I think we can all agree that everyone suffers pain. The first step to dealing with your pain is to evaluate your foundation—your faith, your family, your friends, and your support system. First and foremost, are you drawing closer to God? Are those you're close to willing to listen and be there for you?

The second step is finding things to redirect your thinking away from pain. This does not mean to ignore your pain and the reality of what you're going through. Rather, it's changing your thinking so you can turn your pain into a positive force in your life. Think of your circumstances like a forest fire: even though an out-of-control wildfire is terrible and can cause incredible destruction, a forest fire can also burn away dead growth and allow new life to begin.

The third thing to consider is this: What is the condition of your trust? When you experience a trauma, it will make you go one of two ways—bitter or better. Are you able to trust God that things will get better? Or are you going to remain bitter? Understand that your degree of hope for a better tomorrow means having the grace to forgive others following the trauma of a break-up. If that doesn't happen, you'll grow bitter.

The final key is having a forgiving heart. This is a process, which I will cover more in depth later. You may not be at the point of forgiving your ex-spouse, friends who turned their backs on you, a judge who ruled against you every time, or even your children after they made hurtful comments to you following the marital split. It's when you find yourself forgiving others and not getting upset over the offenses that come against you that you realize God is working on the condition of your heart and setting you on a path toward healing properly.

There are many examples in Scripture where God healed the condition by changing one's perspective. King David is a great example. When you read Psalm 51, you hear David asking God, with great emotion, to give him grace and change his heart.

When you dig a little deeper, you find out that this was David's prayer after the prophet Nathan confronted David's adulteress heart with a story of a rich man who took the sheep of a poor man for his own feast. When David heard Nathan describe what happened, he became very angry and wanted to make the rich man pay for his actions—until Nathan revealed that he was the rich man who took the sheep when he took Uriah's wife, Bathsheba, into the royal bedroom. David was brought low, and that's when his heart changed and he fastened himself to God.

Getting back to Psalm 51, this does not mean that you shouldn't be angry following an offense or not experience bouts of anxiety or depression, which is perfectly normal. Rather, it is not allowing those feelings to guide your actions.

Even Scripture talks about being angry and not sinning. Many people, including myself for a long time, do not understand what it means to be truly angry but not allow that anger to consume you to a point where you lash out and sin. What it means is that you can have feelings about an injustice, but you don't want to allow your emotions to drive you into making rash decisions or poor behavior that you will regret tomorrow.

Part 1:

What does your foundation look like? Read Jesus' words from Matthew 7:24-27 (NIV) below:

> "Therefore everyone who hears these words of mine and puts them into practice is like a wise man who built his house on the rock. The rain came down, the streams rose, and the winds blew and beat against that house; yet it did not fall, because it had its foundation on the rock. But everyone who hears these words of mine and does not put them into practice is like a foolish man who built his house on sand. The rain came down, the streams rose, and the winds blew and beat against that house, and it fell with a great crash."

Ex's & Oh's

After being in the construction business for more than twenty-five years, I have seen my share of foundations that have cracked or sunk or even blown out because of certain conditions or poor construction. What effect has the storm of divorce, separation, or alienation had on your foundation, both physically and mentally?

_____

_____

_____

_____

_____

_____

According to Matthew 7:24-27, the foundation was affected by two factors: erosion and instability. Looking back at the relationships with your ex and your children, do you feel that your foundation was built on shifting sand or on solid rock? (Sometimes in a relationship, it's difficult to see the exact condition of your foundation. It could have been strong, or you may have seen some red flags since hindsight is always 20/20.)

_____

_____

_____

_____

_____

_____

J.K. Nation

Whether you feel your relationship with your kids was built on solid rock or shifting sand, explain how you see the foundation today. Are there any red flags? If so, describe those as well.

_____

_____

_____

_____

_____

_____

What changes would you like to make to shore up your relationships? I'm referring to your ex and your children as well as your friends, neighbors, friends, co-workers and others.

_____

_____

_____

_____

_____

_____

David Brinkley said the key to being a successful individual was laying a firm foundation while others were throwing bricks at you. When I first read this quote, I found Brinkley's words to be profound.

When things are being thrown at you, what are you doing with that? Are you allowing mean comments and hurtful insults to bury you, or are you using them as building blocks to become a better reflection of yourself?

Write down some successes throughout your life and what lead to them. Write down some of the struggles you are dealing with now, including some of the comments that really hurt you. Then come up with a game plan on how you can use these things to become a better reflection of yourself.

_____

_____

_____

_____

_____

_____

It's easy to assume that all is well with the foundation of our relationships. Most of the time, the erosion of a relationship doesn't happen all at once but shifts little by little over time. Before you know it, storms hit and destroy everything you care about. Those are the moments you want to turn to your Father and realize that He is the only foundation that will never fail.

Part 2:

Are your thoughts too consumed by pain? Read Philippians 4:6-9 (NIV) below:

> Do not be anxious about anything, but in every situation, by prayer and petition, with thanksgiving,

present your requests to God. And the peace of God, which transcends all understanding, will guard your hearts and your minds in Christ Jesus.

Finally, brothers and sisters, whatever is true, whatever is noble, whatever is right, whatever is pure, whatever is lovely, whatever is admirable—if anything is excellent or praiseworthy—think about such things. Whatever you have learned or received or heard from me, or seen in me—put it into practice. And the God of peace will be with you.

During a traumatic incident, your thoughts are easily consumed by anxiety, depression, and pain, and sometimes even anger. God doesn't want you to be consumed by negative thoughts because of their adverse impact on your health, the way you carry yourself, and the way you talk to others.

Consider this verse from Psalm 30:5 (NIV)

> For his anger lasts only a moment,
> but his favor lasts a lifetime;
> weeping may stay for the night,
> but rejoicing comes in the morning.

- Of all the thoughts consuming you, which ones do you struggle with the most?

_____

_____

_____

_____

_____

- While going through the legal process of my divorce and separation from my kids, one of the pastors I saw for counseling asked me a simple question nearly every time I saw him. "What does your support group look like?" he asked.

    This is an important question because your support group should have your back as well as be there for accountability. They are the ones you can trust. What does your support group look like? How are they helping you?

    _____

    _____

    _____

    _____

    _____

    _____

- Who should you *not* share intimate details about your struggles? This would include social media or your work environment.

    _____

    _____

    _____

    _____

    _____

    _____

- Has your thinking or any mental setbacks had an adverse effect on your physical health? Write down anything that you may need to see the doctor about. Be cautious about sharing these details about your health.

___

Part 3:

How is your trust? Read Proverbs 3:5-6 (NASB) below:

> Trust in the LORD with all your heart
> And do not lean on your own understanding.
> In all your ways acknowledge Him,
> And He will make your paths straight.

Trust is difficult to give once you've been burned. There's something within us that wants to trust others, especially a spouse, but that can be violated because of cheating, a divorce, or manipulating the relationship between you and the children, which can cause great damage.

- What do you feel broke your trust with your ex? Was trust broken with your extended family and certain friends? If so, describe what that's been like.

- Do you fully trust God with your situation and the aftermath of what you experienced?

- Has your lack of trust in others created bitterness within you?

Not being able to restore your trust in God and others will keep you from healthy relationships with others, including your children, whom you may desire reconciliation with. Just like garlic or onions give you bad breath, so can a lack of trust can lead to bitterness.

Prayer:

Lord God, please examine the condition of my foundation. Show me the areas where I need to forgive others and myself. Allow my thoughts to be more in line with Your thoughts and restore my trust in You and others. In Christ's name, amen.

Additional Scriptures to dwell on throughout the week:

- Psalm 34:18 (NKJV): The LORD is near to those who have a broken heart, and saves such as have a contrite spirit.
- Matthew 18:21-22 (NKJV): Then Peter came to Him and said, "Lord, how often shall my brother sin against me, and I forgive him? Up to seven times?" Jesus said to him, "I do not say to you, up to seven times, but up to seventy times seven."
- Psalm 30:11, 12 (NIV): You turned my wailing into dancing; you removed my sackcloth and clothed me with joy, that my heart may sing your praises and not be silent. LORD my God, I will praise you forever.

Journal:

_____

_____

_____

_____

7

Praying and Seeking Restoration in the Home

> "Emphasize reconciliation, not resolution. It is unrealistic to expect everyone to agree about everything. Reconciliation focuses on the relationship, while resolution focuses on the problem. When we focus on reconciliation, the problem loses significance and often becomes irrelevant."
> —Rick Warren, author of the best-selling *The Purpose Driven Life*

This is one of the hardest chapters for me to write because I have struggled with what restoration and reconciliation looks like between me and my children. I can still remember some of the questions I've asked myself over the years:

- "What can I expect after all of the dust settles?"
- "Is God big enough to take my broken pieces and make something beautiful out of them?"
- "If I have a relationship again with my kids, what will that look like? Will they accept me and love me as their parent?"
- "Will I ever get past the hurt and pain? Or will all my pain and hurt come flooding back the next time I get the opportunity to see them again?"

From early in my marriage, I always desired to be a father. Becoming a parent was granted to me, not by any person, but rather as a God-given blessing. Most people do not see their children as a blessing; instead, they view their children as just another part of life.

That's not the right attitude to have. We should never take for granted how children are a blessing from the Lord, which is why divorce can be so damaging. If you've gone through a marital breakup like I have, then you haven't forgotten the voices of your children calling out "Daddy" with excited squeaky voices or those times where they nestled in your arms and looked at you for comfort and affirmation.

Then, for whatever reason or explanation, your babies are no longer in your life and the hole in your heart is indescribable. Nonetheless, you can't wait for the day when you can say to your children, "Yes, I approve of you and love you with all of my being."

Shortly after my divorce, my prayer to God was that one day there would be restoration between me and my children. As months turned into years, however, I had many nights where I could not sleep and many days where I felt I could not function. I poured out my heart to God, telling Him that I was broken beyond repair. As the words rolled from my lips, I heard God tell me this:

I have brought you beyond broken. I have brought you beyond crushed. I have ground you into powder. In your brokenness I can make you into limited things, but when you are crushed into powder, I can add the water of my Holy Spirit and make you brand new, into something you weren't before. I do this so you can be a testimony through this journey.

It's easy to think that because we are crushed, we end up loosing our usefulness. I reflect on the story of Abraham in the Bible where God gave him a blessing—his son Isaac—only to ask him to sacrifice his only hope for the future on an altar. Sometimes God will bring us to a point where what we had hoped for must be given back to Him to change our dependence on things to depending on Him.

I liken our brokenness to building a foundation. Foundations are usually made from concrete, and one of the characteristics of concrete is that it can be recycled and made into a new foundation. There are two forms of concrete can be made during the recycling process. Concrete can be turned into a gravel or dry aggregate, but the process to achieve either one is quite different.

To make gravel, you need to break up the old concrete into smaller parts, removing any metal but not all imperfections. Creating an aggregate, though, requires two additional steps: sifting the contaminates out and crushing the old concrete into powder. When water is mixed in, the aggregate can be used as new concrete to create a new foundation.

Too often we see the foundation that we built during the marriage crack and crumble, but we don't see the contaminates that caused our foundation to fail. We look to God and ask Him to patch up the cracked foundation, hoping that will take care of the problem, but like an engineer, God requires the foundation to be replaced with materials stronger and better than before.

He looks at it and says, *I'm going to sift the contaminates, take out the remnants, and make something newer and stronger than before. Do you trust Me?* Unless you trust that God knows what He is doing, you will never see the bigger picture of His plan for your life and will be left with a broken foundation and lots of rubble.

When many see their foundation crumbing around them, they tend to lose their identity because they put their faith in what they built—like marrying and having kids—and expected God to bless their efforts. For me, being a husband and father was so important that I did not see the imperfections I was adding to the foundation and wanted—or expected—God to bless my family life in the process. The disintegration of my marriage required me to take a step back and see just how God was going to restore me through building a new foundation in my life.

As I think about the journey I've been on, I had to see God as my Father and Someone who knew what He was doing. I needed to hear Him say, *I love you and am proud of you for making your way through this journey, which has been really tough. So, know this: I believe in you.*

God looks at us the way I looked at my sons when I could watch them play youth baseball—which was awesome—or when my daughter shook hands with a U.S. congressman after winning an art award. Today, I better understand that I can't make it totally on my own, but if I stay the course, loving my children as God loves me, in good times and in bad times, then restoration is not only attainable, but restoration will feel like sweet healing. This is what God has always desired for me and my family as well as for you and your children.

God sees your heart and understands your desires. He knows what He desires in your family and in your life. It's perfectly fine to tell God of your brokenness, leaving those pieces at His feet and standing back while He creates a new foundation and a masterpiece of new construction from the shards of your journey. Don't lose hope because He promises to be there for you, your children, and your children's children.

Part 1:

When it comes to praying and seeking restoration in your home, the concept may be a confusing one, but peace and harmony is not a pipe dream. Romans 12:18 (NKJV) says it best:

> If possible, so far as it depends on you, be at peace with all men.

There are two things about this verse from Romans that makes this line of Scripture so important. The first is that you have the option and power to find restoration. The second is God knows what is in your best interest.

Read Deuteronomy 30:1-5 (MSG). Can you relate with any part of these verses?

> Here's what will happen. While you're out among the nations where God has dispersed you and the blessings and curses come in just the way I have set them before you, and you and your children take them seriously and come back to God, your God, and obey him with your whole heart and soul according to everything that I command you today, God, your God, will restore everything you lost; he'll have compassion on you; he'll come back and pick up the pieces from all the places where you were

scattered. No matter how far away you end up, God, your God, will get you out of there and bring you back to the land your ancestors once possessed. It will be yours again. He will give you a good life and make you more numerous than your ancestors.

- Do you feel like your life has been dispersed because of where your journey has taken you? Explain what "scattering" looks like and how it has effected your perspective on life's big decisions.

_____

_____

_____

_____

_____

_____

_____

Restoration:

This is how the dictionary defines the word *restoration:*

- "The act or process of returning something to its original condition by repairing it, cleaning it, etc." (desire to fix what is broken where there is peace)
- "The act of bringing back something that existed before" (desire for what was in the past)
- "The act of returning something that was stolen or taken" (to find justice in the situation)

Looking at the definitions of the word *restoration*, which definition do you relate with the most? Those who have gone through severe Parental Alienation may state that all three fit their definition of restoration. After all, these parents have experienced the desire to have the broken fixed and find peace. They also long for justice and the good days of long ago. What are your feelings?

_____

_____

_____

_____

_____

_____

- If you could describe what restoration would look like in your current situation, how would you express that? Share some of your thoughts here.

_____

_____

_____

_____

_____

_____

- We all have broken pieces in life. Sometimes looking at those pieces results in holding on to them for too long because they represent what ~~we~~ you once had. What do your broken pieces look like?

    Other times, restoration requires God to reduce the things you have built, including your expectations, and turning that into a powder that has removed any contaminates in order to make something new. Have you asked God to create something new with what you once had? You can, you know.

    _____

    _____

    _____

    _____

    _____

    _____

- Just like a forest fire burns everything—the good and the bad—all is not lost. Sooner or later, new growth will sprout up. Have you seen any new growth happen yet? If so, what does it look like? Are you feeling positive about the direction you're heading?

    _____

    _____

    _____

    _____

    _____

    _____

- Everyone knows that a parent's approval is very important to children. Your children will always need to hear you express your unconditional love for them, regardless of their age, how far they live from you, or the amount of time that you've been apart.

  Likewise, allow God to love you so that you can heal and understand what true restoration looks like. He wants to comfort you. Draw close to Him, nestle in His lap, and let Him wrap His arms around you. He will let you know that you're going to be okay.

  Do you see God in the same role you're trying to be to your children? Are you drawing close to Him? If so, how can you tell?

_____

_____

_____

_____

_____

_____

_____

Part 2:

When it comes to understanding reconciliation, author and pastor Rick Warren says there's a great misconception about reconciliation and that too often people will attack each other, not as an attempt to seek reconciliation, but to find some sort of way to resolve their issues.

- When you look at reconciliation, are you looking at restoring your relationship or resolving your problems, including all the pain and baggage involved? If it's the latter, what is some of the baggage that needs to be resolved? What's keeping you from taking steps to restore your relationship at least partially?

_____

_____

_____

_____

_____

- What is the most important issue that's keeping you from taking steps toward some sort of reconciliation? If you could resolve a few things, do you think you can move on? If so, what would that look like?

_____

_____

_____

_____

_____

It's easy to get caught in the trap of thinking *If I put this situation or relationship behind me, then I will have bigger and better things on the horizon.* The reality is God created us for relationship, and in doing so, He has given us tools to seek restoration to avert future pain.

Over the years people have told me that I need to move on rather than seek any sort of reconciliation with my ex or my past. I've found that moving on means resolving to forget about the past pain, as impossible as that's been. Eventually, as I've noticed, certain things came seeping back, but not much could be done about that.

So what I've done instead of "moving on" is to "move forward," which is the act of processing through a problem rather than forgetting about it. Maybe it's time for you to move forward instead of moving on.

Challenge:

Remember, any restoration that happens—whether it's with your ex and/or your children—is not just for you but for generations to come, so be patient with your circumstances. Of course, this is easier said than done, but let your life be a testament of His goodness in your life.

Prayer:

Lord God, give us an understanding of Your bigger picture. Take my broken pieces and make a masterpiece out of my mess today. Allow me not to lose hope in the hard times and to remember Your promise of restoration for my family. Protect my children and my children's children from the pain I have had to suffer. More importantly, make my life be a standing stone where generations can see Your faithfulness and see that You brought me through a raging river that looked impossible to cross. Lord, I stand for the promise You have for generations to come, which is that they may praise Your name. In the name of Jesus, amen.

Additional Scriptures to dwell on throughout the week:

Deuteronomy 30:1-5: for a reminder that God will restore you, have mercy on you, and gather you back.

Joshua 4:7: for a reminder of the stones that stand as a memorial for the people of Israel.

Joshua 24:15: for a reminder that you are to the serve the Lord, not others.

Journal:

8
Talking About Forgiveness

> "Nothing is sweeter than the day we call out for forgiveness."
> —TobyMac, contemporary Christian music artist

What is forgiveness, and how does the act of forgiving fit into the context of post-divorce and Parental Alienation?

I know that raising the idea of forgiving your ex makes this a very difficult chapter to read, but this is probably the most important chapter in this book. Truth is, I've struggled greatly with this topic. It took me a year-and-a-half of writing and rewriting my thoughts before I felt I was ready to share this.

First off, forgiveness and peace seem to go hand in hand and be intentional to do. The question is: How do you forgive someone who has violated you or taken away something that was yours?

Too often what keeps us from forgiving others stems from how much the violation affected us. What they did is a stumbling block and stops us from seeing the bigger picture about why forgiveness is important and what it can help us achieve in life. On the other hand, unforgiveness becomes a crutch or justification for how we feel toward someone, which, in turn, keeps us from the promises God has for our lives.

When it comes to forgiving others, I want to share an important verse of Scripture to set the right tone. This comes from Romans 12:18 (NKJV):

> If it is possible, as far as it depends on you, live at peace with everyone.

Now take a look at how Romans 12:18 is written in the Message version:

> Don't hit back; discover beauty in everyone. If you've got it in you, get along with everybody. Don't insist on getting even; that's not for you to do. "I'll do the judging," says God. "I'll take care of it."

As I have wrestled with this factor of forgiveness, I had to start by breaking down the word *forgiveness*, which is a combination of two separate words:

- **for:** "to do something with an objective or purpose."
- **give:** "to present voluntarily and without expecting compensation."

When you put these two words together, you get this:

- **forgive:** "the deliberate act of giving to someone without the expectation of being compensated."

As I took this in, I put it to the litmus test of my divorce and my journey. That was tough to do.

As I have revealed throughout *Ex's & Oh's*, I tried everything in my power to get my parental rights reinstated. I went through the courts. I went through counseling. I attempted to reconcile with my ex-wife and kids to no avail.

But imagine if the key to unlocking the door was found in something entirely different—through forgiveness, not by words or a legal decision but rather by action? Imagine if all I had to do to put this behind me was to make a conscious decision to live in peace with others without expectation of anything in return?

As I worked through my feelings and contemplated what to share in this chapter, I heard my pastor talk about how to "dance in the rain." He said this when he preached from Psalm 23. When I listened to him explain the psalm's six verses, I could not believe how imperative those verses were and what they had to do with forgiveness.

Let's look at Psalm 23 (NASB) together:

> The Lord is my shepherd,
> I shall not want.
> He makes me lie down in green pastures;
> He leads me beside quiet waters.
> He restores my soul;
> He guides me in paths of righteousness
> For His name's sake.
> Even though I walk through the valley of the shadow of death,
> I fear no evil, for You are with me;
> Your rod and staff, they comfort me.
> You prepare a table before me in the presence of my enemies;
> You anointed my head with oil;
> My cup overflows.
> Surely goodness and loving kindness will follow me all the days of my life,
> And I will dwell in the house of the Lord forever.

It was verse 5 that popped out to me:

> You prepare a table before me in the presence of my enemies.

What I thought about was that we go through life and encounter people who may at one time intended to bring blessings into our lives, but something happened to make everything go off the rails. For some reason, that person became our number one adversary. Maybe it's an ex-spouse, family member, friend, or just someone from our community.

Imagine what would happen if you could win over that person who turned into your enemy? Would you do it? Would you attempt to become a peacemaker? If you could win your kids back and open communication with them after a dry spell, would you give in to your ex and trust God that He will make things right in His way?

Look at the second part of Psalm 23:5 and verse 6:

> You anointed my head with oil;
> My cup overflows.
> Surely goodness and loving kindness will follow me
> all the days of my life,
> And I will dwell in the house of the Lord forever.

In the Jewish tradition, particularly in ancient times, oil was very important and was used for one of four things, which made it one of the most valuable commodities in the ancient world. Those four uses were cooking, healing, as fuel to light a room, and for anointing of royalty. In this verse, oil was used for each of these acts.

If you decide to forgive someone and live according to Romans 12:18 while acknowledging Psalm 23:5's counsel to become a "peacemaker" and reside in peace with others, let me remind you about the second part of that Scripture verse that leaves you with a promise: "You have anointed my head with oil; my cup overflows" (Psalm 23:5b).

Suppose that through your process of forgiveness God marks you with His blessing, and by that, I mean restoration. But that's not all! Imagine that your restoration is so sweet that it brings you healing, feeds your soul, gives you joy, and lights each room you walk into along your journey. Imagine if your willingness to seek peace overflowed to your ex and from your ex to your kids and from your kids to your grandkids and so on.

Wouldn't that make it worth being a peacemaker? Doesn't that paint a new picture of hope where something radical could take place—so radical that you could actually enjoy the preverbal "thanksgiving" banquet in the presence of your one-time enemy?

Part 1:

So, having heard my thoughts, what does forgiveness mean to you? Here's Psalm 23 (NASB) again:

> The Lord is my shepherd,
> I shall not want.
> He makes me lie down in green pastures;
> He leads me beside quiet waters.

> He restores my soul;
> He guides me in paths of righteousness
> For His name's sake.
> Even though I walk through the valley of the shadow of death,
> I fear no evil, for You are with me;
> Your rod and staff, they comfort me.
> You prepare a table before me in the presence of my enemies;
> You anointed my head with oil;
> My cup overflows.
> Surely goodness and loving kindness will follow me all the days of my life,
> And I will dwell in the house of the Lord forever.

Forgiveness is a difficult choice for anyone to carry out, but your decision to forgive can free you from pain, sorrow, regret, and anger. Knowing that, wouldn't the act of forgiveness be worth its weight in gold?

Please understand that this does not mean that you step back into the abuse you may have received in the past. Rather, it's a release of the pain and anger associated with a bad experience and finding healthy boundaries that will help you thrive and allow God to restore you.

Moving forward, consider these questions:

- When you read Psalm 23, how does it change your perspective regarding forgiveness?

_____

_____

_____

_____

_____

- At the beginning of this chapter, I shared a verse in Romans about becoming a peacemaker and living in peace with others. How would you define what a "peacemaker" is and what his or her role looks like?

___

- What obstacles make it difficult for you to forgive your ex-spouse (or extended family members or others)? Don't hesitate to write about a number of them if there are many.

___

- When looking at Psalm 23:5, what does "You prepare a table before me in the presence of my enemies" look like to you?

___

_____

_____

_____

_____

Part 2:

Music has been an integral part of my life and a great way for me to cope with setbacks. Many artists have put out songs dealing with things like hope and love, but very few have dealt with forgiveness. A notable example is a song called "Forgiveness" by the Christian artist TobyMac.

- Go online and listen to the song. What is TobyMac's song saying to you?

_____

_____

_____

_____

_____

_____

Music can help you through the process of this journey. Here are some titles of songs and artists that have helped me along the way. I strongly encourage you to listen to each of these songs and see how they can resonate with you.

- "Won't Stop Now" by Elevation Worship
- "Don't Worry Now" by Britt Nicole

- "Haven't Seen It Yet" by Danny Gokey
- "Here Again" by Elevation Worship
- "Hope in Front of Me" by Danny Gokey
- "See You Again" by Carrie Underwood
- "Through It All" by Colton Dixon

Music can bring hope, healing, and resolve to keep going in the midst of tough times.

Part 3:

Who do you need to forgive? Read Matthew 6:14-15 (MSG) below:

> In prayer there is a connection between what God does and what you do. You can't get forgiveness from God, for instance, without also forgiving others. If you refuse to do your part, you cut yourself off from God's part.

Let me be the first to say that forgiveness has been difficult for me. The offenses I have had to deal with because of my divorce and separation from my kids made things tough, which means that forgiveness was a process.

Each day I had to "choose" to forgive, and sometimes I had to choose to forgive several times a day or a week. Sure, there were plenty of areas that never got fully resolved and I had to contend with a flood of emotions.

- What do you need to forgive regarding your ex? How have you been wronged?

_____

_____

_____

- If you're going through a Parental Alienation issue, you may have had insults and hurtful comments thrown at you by your children. Do you hold unforgiveness towards your children? What's that been like for you?

- One of the hardest things to do is to forgive someone who's hurt you, especially someone who hurt you out of spite. But what about yourself? Is there something you need to forgive yourself for? This could be harsh words you've said in the past, substance abuse, or wrong thinking.

_____

_____

_____

_____

Challenge:

In the construction field, when a foundation cracks or fails, it must be underpinned. It is only when you underpin a foundation that can you address any hairline cracks by patching, tuck pointing, and filling in the gaps. Understand that underpinning is not there to highlight the problems but rather to make something old new again. Normally the process of underpinning, if done correctly, is hidden and behind the scenes.

One of the things I found helpful as an act of underpinning was to do something for someone else. I had many people talk to me about the grief that they were suffering from and the consuming fear they felt when their children's birthdays came around. I know by experience the depression and anxiety I felt each time one of my kids had a birthday. It wasn't difficult to feel bitter about the place I was in.

I found the best way to work through the depression and anxiety I felt was by doing something for someone else. In doing so, I was preparing my heart for a time of reconciliation with my kids and blessing along the way.

That hasn't happened yet but doing random acts of kindness for others has helped me tremendously. I urge you to give it a try. Here are some suggestions of things you could do to change your thinking, which will help in the underpinning process of dealing with the pain and healing properly. My advice requires stepping out of your element, but once you do, you can begin to trust again:

- As a father and being subtracted from my kids' lives, I found that mentoring other kids was important to me. One of the things that hurt deeply for me was no longer being an active father after

my kids were taken away. Maybe you can help out in children's church, coach a baseball or football team, or ask one of the schools in the area (preferably not your children's school if the courts have removed your parental rights) if you can be part of an after-school tutoring program.
- Helping out at a nursing home. The elderly have all the time to listen to you, so it's a win-win for everyone: they enjoy the company, and you can learn more about who you are.
- Volunteering at a shelter, hospital, or a community center. Reaching out in this capacity can allow you to share your story with others and bring hope to someone else struggling.
- Joining a support group.

Prayer:

Lord God, please teach me more about forgiveness and allow me to experience the act of forgiving more freely. Allow me to understand that the act of forgiveness is a conscious decision that brings restoration. When someone wrongs me, let me decisively give with the purpose of not getting anything back. When I am in the spirit to not forgive, please remind me how You intentionally stretched out Your arms to forgive me of my trespasses. Lord God, teach me a deeper understanding of restoration. In the name of Jesus, amen.

Additional Scriptures to dwell on throughout the week:

- Colossians 3:13, which talks about making allowance for each other's faults.
- Matthew 6:14-15, which reminds you that if you refuse to forgive others, God will not forgive your sins.
- Ephesians 4:31-32, which reminds you to get rid of all bitterness and anger and to be kind and forgiving of one another.
- 1 John 1:9, which says that if we confess our sins to Him, He will be faithful and forgive us of our sins.

Journal:

9 Starting New Goals and Dreams

> "If you fail to plan, you are planning to fail."
> —Benjamin Franklin, one of the Founding Fathers of the United States

Hearing someone talk about goals and dreams may sound like a cliché, especially if your goals and dreams were shattered by divorce.

It's important, though, no matter if you're divorced, married, or still single, to think about your future and the direction God has for your life. And no matter what happened to you, you still have a future, which means you can still have hopes and goals and dreams.

From my early days or working in the construction industry, I used Jeremiah 29:11-14 (NIV) as my key verses for my business. Let's review them here:

> "For I know the plans I have for you,' declares the Lord, 'I plans to prosper you and not to harm you, plans to give you a hope and a future. Then you will call on me and come and pray to me, and I will listen to you. You will seek me and find me when you seek me with all your heart. I will be found by you,' declares the Lord, 'and bring you back from captivity. I will gather you from all the nations and the places where I have banished you,' declares the Lord, 'and I will bring you back to the place from where I carried you into exile."

I never realized the impact these Scripture verses would have on my life, especially early on in my divorce when I felt very lost. That was a bleak period when I did not know how to overcome depression, anxiety, hurt, and anger.

One time, one of my friends reached out and invited me to a nutrition and chiropractic conference. As I walked into the church where the symposium was being held at, a song played in the background. I recognized it: "Moving Forward" by Ricardo Sanchez.

This stirring song stopped me dead in my tracks, and I felt nothing less than paralyzed. You see, for the year and a half—and sometimes even today—people would tell me that I just needed to move on. My response would invariably be this: "Do you have any idea what it's been like to not only go through a divorce after being married for thirteen years, but on top of that, have my kids taken away from me, which were an integral part of my life and identity?"

Those who heard me say this agreed I had a point, and I did feel some sort of resolution after hearing "Moving Forward" that day. What was happening was that I was receiving the answer I needed: It was not a matter of moving on rather a matter of moving forward. The next time well-meaning people told me, "You just need to move on," I reminded myself that you just don't just "move on" from having four kids and completely disconnecting from your past and experiences. But I could move forward.

God doesn't call us to forget our past but to *forgive* our past and hinge our identity on Him.

Up until my marriage blew apart, I realized that my identity was defined: being financially successful, having a strong marriage and lifelong partner, and raising children and grandchildren who loved the Lord and would impact the world. In just over a year, though, everything I had dreamed of and aspired to was wiped out.

The housing market plummeted, and I had to close my construction design business because clients failed to pay me. I lost my brand-new car, which wasn't a good thing for the marriage, and a few short months later, a tropical storm sat over our area, dumping 26 inches of rain and flooding our house, forcing us into bankruptcy and having to move twice. To add insult to injury, I could not find work and got very ill. Then the trifecta happened: my wife left and took our kids.

I mentioned earlier that I felt like Job, but actually was more like Joseph, who had his life upended when his jealous brothers sold him into slavery in Egypt to get rid of him. I, in no way, want to compare what I went through to the deprivation that Joseph experienced in Egypt many millennia ago, but I'm a survivor and attribute my survival to calling on the Lord during this tough time. That's why, a decade later, I can honestly state that it's critical to hold fast to two truths:

1. God is good.
2. His mercies are new every morning.

Remind yourself of these two truths, and you will learn how to move forward and not move on.

Jeremiah 29:11-14 are great verses to live by during deep and traumatic times when it's easy to spiral out of control and fail to see the plans God has for you. Anyone living in the midst of a chaotic period will tell you how difficult it is to find the right direction in life, so think about it this way. Imagine driving on a highway in an ice storm at rush hour. An SUV slides into a sedan just ahead of you, and suddenly you see all sorts of cars and trucks spinning out of control in front of you and in your rearview mirror.

What do you do? It's natural to react rather than be strategic, but if you can become more strategic in your response, you can minimize tragedy.

In the case of an icy highway, the strategic response would be to slow down when the roads are icy and maintain plenty of distance between you and the cars ahead of you instead of hoping that you can react in time if there's a crash in front of you. There's no guarantee you'll stop in time, but by strategically slowing down and keeping your distance from other cars, you greatly reduce the chances of a tragic accident occurring.

So how can you be more strategic when your world is turning into one big wreck all around you? I know what I'm about to say may sound simple, but the answer is hidden in plain sight in these verses from Jeremiah. God desires you to call on Him and seek Him wholeheartedly now—before tragedy hits. When you call on Him now, it's like you're saying to Him during a big snowstorm on the interstate, "Here, You take the wheel. You keep me safe."

It's easy to focus on the damage happening around you, but when you understand God's perspective in the middle of the chaos, you can rest assured that His plans are not for tragedy but rather for protection. Just like in the accident, you can look at the damage around you or look at what God has done to protect you in the process.

Another way I can explain it is through the parent/child relationship. As you know, your kids look to you for stability, protection, and provision. As they get older and reach the preteen and teen years, they strive for independence and often feel they have all the answers. They will often fight and argue with you for their "freedom."

When they fight to remove themselves from your protection, so to speak, it's like they're insisting on driving in icy conditions when they'd be better off letting you remain behind the wheel because of your experience in snowy conditions. Sure, there will be a time when their old enough and experienced to drive in inclement weather, but until then, they should realize that they will be better off calling on you for protection.

Part 1:

Identify your original goals by reading Luke 14:28-30 (NIV):

> "Suppose one of you wants to build a tower. Won't you first sit down and estimate the cost to see if you have enough money to complete it? For if you lay the foundation and are not able to finish it, everyone who sees it will ridicule you say, 'This person began to build and wasn't able to finish.'"

In Central Florida, there is a building some call "The Eyesore on I-4."

Nearly twenty years ago, some Christian investors decided that they would build the "Majesty Building" in Altamonte Springs right next to Interstate 4. At the time, the investors took donations to build the structure. When the donations stopped and the economy tanked, construction stopped. The building to this day sits empty and is only 80 percent complete.

Many of us go through life like the Majesty Building. You have good intentions to do amazing things and patiently wait for people to invest in you. And then one tragic day, something happens. You get hit with a trauma: it could be divorce, a death in the family, a financial falling out, or failing health. You're paralyzed and unable to keep building, to move forward.

People you know see you in your unfinished or broken state, and they assume that you couldn't finish what you set out to do. The truth is the trauma was too great to continue in the same course you once had. Sometimes what's needed is for someone to come alongside and help you finish.

After the Stoneman Douglas High School shooting in Parkland, Florida, in 2018, I heard an interesting interview with a teacher from Columbine High School in Colorado. She was at Columbine during their school shooting in 1999.

"Once someone experiences trauma, especially in a child, it rewires their thinking," the thoughtful teacher said. "What once made sense and was just part of everyday life is now scrutinized. It could be a smell, a slamming door, or the backfire of a car that makes you relive that tragic time and makes you revert. This was something we did not understand with Columbine and just thought the kids would bounce back, but we know differently today."

What a profound statement! Each tragedy can have triggers that brings you back to the tragedy again, which can cripple you and stop you from moving forward. I know for me that the biggest triggers are hearing certain songs. The melodies instantly transport me to a certain time and certain memories that are not always good for me. When I feel that happening, I remind myself that's in the past and I need to move forward.

- Before you can move forward, seek to identify some of the hurdles in front of you. Think about some of the goals you started with but never finished due to some type of tragedy. List them below.

_____

_____

- What are some things holding you back from finishing those goals you started? What could you do to get off the dime?

- List some ways you can retool or recast your original goals to help you finish what you started.

One more thought: It's important to finish a goal, even if your original interest is lacking. If old goals sit unfinished, however, that could set a pattern to not finish future goals.

Part 2:

When it comes to turning lemons into lemonade, it's human nature to dwell on your pain, problems, or trauma or simply avoid them all together to avoid future pain. What can you take from these difficult or bad circumstances and turn them into your strengths and successes? Instead of avoiding them, can you take the opportunity to learn from your experiences and experience a new success?

When I mentioned there were songs that triggered pain, one group I avoided was Casting Crowns. This was because the last time I saw my kids just prior to my divorce, my ex wanted my boys to stop playing youth baseball on a team I was coaching and put them in a play that featured Casting Crowns music.

That really bothered me. I felt she was doing this for her benefit and not allowing the kids to do what they wanted to or were committed to. Each time I heard a Casting Crowns song come on the radio or through my Pandora app, I remembered what she did to separate me from my children.

The interesting thing is there was a Casting Crowns song that really ministered to me called "Already There." This song seemed to be my prayer and cry to God when I heard the lyrics. I could not understand how God would use a group I deliberately avoided to bring me healing, but He did.

While talking to God about having reconciliation with my kids, He asked me, *Do you trust me? Do you trust that reconciliation may not look like you want or expect? Do you realize that reconciliation can be fulfilled completely through your grandchildren?*

In the back story of "Already There," Casting Crowns lead singer Mark Hall said, "God is not looking to steer you off a cliff. God is already sitting on the porch with you and your wife, watching your grandkids."

That's a major wow. These days, years later, God has taken me out of my element and pain and not replaced my kids, but He's brought salve to the soul where there was once a great bleeding sore. He has brought things like mentoring other children to bring joy where there was once pain.

Unless we allow God to reach us and push through the bad things, we cannot experience the healing we need to transform our lives. Sometimes it requires you to take a deep look at where you came from and subject those memories to a different perspective. It may require you to relive the pain you have so desperately tried to avoid and make yourself vulnerable again. Until you do that, you will be limited in how much you can move forward in life as well as in other relationships.

- So, moving forward, what are some things that you would classify as the lemons in your life that that caused you great pain and have been avoiding? Examples could be going to certain places, eating certain foods, celebrating certain traditions, socializing with certain people, or listening to certain songs.

_____

_____

_____

_____

_____

- Once you have identified your "lemons," try to write down a different perspective of those things you have been avoiding. List some redemptive things you could say about these things.

_____

_____

_____

- How can you take these things that were once your pain and turn them into something rewarding and redemptive? How can they become a blessing to you and others?

Part 3:

When it comes to making new goals, sometimes traumas can be blessings in disguise. For example, if you were in a bad marriage where you did not finish your education, you could have the opportunity, time, and ability to finish your education. Or maybe you can slow down a bit and reset and recharge. Whatever your situation, you may be entering an unusual period in your life where you can start new routines and do something you otherwise might not have done.

When inventor Thomas Edison was asked about his failures, he responded the following: "I have not failed. I've just found 10,000 ways that don't work."

Not only did Edison struggle with failure, but he also he struggled with physical disabilities. Born in 1847 and raised in Port Huron, Michigan, Edison wasn't able to read or comprehend due to dyslexia, which was later compounded by losing 80 percent of his hearing due to scarlet fever as a teen. These afflictions didn't stop Edison from striving for his goals and desires. Rather, he turned them into strengths that led him to patent more inventions than anyone in history—more than 2,300, including the light bulb, motion picture camera, and phonograph.

Are you allowing failures or setbacks to define our direction? This is not the time to quit or collapse, placing your dreams aside and not forward in life.

- So here's my question: What setbacks in life or failures are holding you back from achieving your goals?

_____

_____

_____

_____

_____

_____

- If you had a clean slate with nothing weighing you down, what goals would you have? Don't be afraid to dream big. Sometimes writing down goals help you plan a direction for where you want to go.

_____

_____

_____

- How can you achieve these goals? List some ways that will help you achieve them.

_____

_____

_____

_____

_____

_____

Challenge:

It's highly important to set goals because they are the blueprint of your life. You may not fulfill every goal you aspire to, but having goals gives you direction on what your next steps should be. Just like in the building of a house, you must have a set of plans to guide you as you build.

Sometimes things work out exactly as drawn up, and other times there are slight variations. When you look at the entire plan, though, you have a far greater chance of completing your building without getting sidetracked because you know what the final result should be.

Too often, life throws you curveballs to the point where you're ready to burn down the structure. Keep in mind what your long-term goal is and realize that things may change, and if something unexpected comes up, it's not the end of the world.

As you pray for God to help you establish and fulfill your goals, dwell on the additional scriptural verses below and see what God has to say to you. Ask Him for opportunities and creativity as you seek direction in your life.

Final Thoughts:

In 1988, when an earthquake killed over 25,000 people in Armenia, a story of survival came out.

A father dropped off his son at school prior to the earthquake. Shortly after the tremblor, he returned to the spot where he left his son. To his dismay, the school was flattened by the tragic earthquake. For the next thirty-six hours, the father dug to try to find his son. Many onlookers thought he was digging out of grief.

At the thirty-sixth hour, he heard a sound. Others helped him move away rubble, and together they found his son and twelve other youngsters. The son attested to the others that his father would come for them, which gave them the hope they needed to stay alive and be reunited again with their loved ones.

Too often, we expect everything to go well without fault, but when the earth quakes and shakes our very existence, we must either dig or heed the calls to give up. We must make a choice. Many assume that they are always like the Armenian father, digging for their child. The reality is we are the children waiting on God to dig us out and reunite us in relationship with Him.

Although those dealing with Parental Alienation gave a set desire to be reunited with our children, the truth is that our difficulties are reuniting us with our God! When the Lord gets our attention with the earthquakes of life, it's to restore our relationship with Him in order to exceed our relationship with others, including our children, for the legacy He has for us.

Prayer:

Lord God, revive my eyes that I may see that those things I have experienced are a piece of Your larger plan. Change my perspective that I may see above those things that distract me from the plans you have for my life. When chaos comes before me, allow me to enjoy the banquet table You have set for me in the presence of my enemies. May my eyes always be set in an upward perspective. In the name of Jesus, amen.

Additional Scriptures to dwell on throughout the week:

- Jeremiah 33:3: The Lord says when you call on Him, He will answer you and tell you great things you don't know.
- Luke 14:28-30: In these verses, Jesus says if you're going to build a tower, be sure to estimate the cost so that you'll have enough money to finish it.
- Psalm 23: This often-quote Scripture reminds us that the Lord is our shepherd and that we lack nothing.

Journal:

_____

_____

_____

_____

_____

_____

_____

_____

_____

Acknowledgements

As I think of this journey and all of those who have been an influence to this book, I cannot help but think of all those who have been by my side for nearly five years to create the content on these pages.

First and foremost, I must give all thanks and gratitude to my Savior Jesus Christ. Without Him being by my side, I know I would have been crushed beyond my limits. Although I never wanted this process, He has been my comfort, healing, blessing, and the One who has held me in dark times and reminded me just how much He loved me.

There are many I would like to thank personally for the influence they have had on my life and for giving me the courage and strength to bring out this book. Without these many family and friends by my side, I would not be where I am today, and I thank you for all you have done and the little parts you have had to make a difference in my life.

I want to thank my parents as they have been a blessing and a cornerstone planting the seed of faith. I also want to thank my children for being the catalyst in my life and challenging me to have a new perspective. I love you very much and that will never change.

Most importantly I want to thank My Girl for being by my side in this dark journey. You have been my inspiration and have seen my highs and lows first hand. You have been the one who breathed life back into me when I was in my worst state, who walked alongside me for many years, and who inspired me to keep going even in the hardest times. You have seen God transform me from where I was to where He has been bringing me. I love you very much!

I also want to thank my editor as he has been such an amazing help and influence bringing the best out of me onto these pages. You have taught me a lot and, in turn, showed me things about myself I could not see.

Finally, I want to thank Westbow Press for taking the opportunity to bring forward such an important book to bring healing for all those who may read this book. May my effort bring people to a closer relationship with God.

I know there are many others that I may have forgotten, but may God be glorified because of your faithfulness. May you strive in His grace.

About the Author

Being a father of four children and going through a messy divorce, I have learned some important things along the way on how to survive the process. Being separated from any communication from your kids with little to no visitation or communication for nearly a decade can be a nearly impossible thing as it takes your hope and joy. As a result, I had to cling to God's promises of reconciliation and a deeper relationship with God as his father. Due to the dark journey I would like to share with others how to survive and find joy again.

To understand where the passion and desire to write this book came from, I must take you back on my journey which started in November of 2009. Suffering a great loss in the construction field, the south was decimated pushing me into bankruptcy. If that wasn't bleak enough, the only asset I thought we could keep, our house, was damaged by a tropical storm.

Due to the losses, we went from our beautiful home with our four children to a tight apartment. The trauma that hit created a toll on my family and marriage. During this time, I was also suffering from some health issues limiting the amount of work I could do and sending my wife back out into the work world again after being a stay-at-home mother for nearly 12 years.

In November of 2009 my marriage was haunted by what would be a very ugly divorce. As a result, I have had my highs and lows, mountain top experiences as well as dark lonely valleys. One truth I learned is that although others may leave you, God can see you through in the most difficult times.

Most ask if the journey can be real and how one can survive if it were. The reality is unless you have lived it, you may never understand the deep loss and pain. As a result, I have clung to my faith and learned new truths to navigate the dark valley referred to in Psalm 23 and would like to take you on a journey for your healing. Through the process I found I am not defined by my situation rather by God's grace.

CPSIA information can be obtained
at www.ICGtesting.com
Printed in the USA
LVHW090926191119
637846LV00001B/2/P